WEIRD IS THE NEW NORMAL

WEIRD IS THE NEW NORMAL
the unlikely path of leadership

MICHAEL MEYER

Copyright © 2025 Michael Meyer and M31 Group

All rights reserved. No part of this publication may be reproduced, distributed, or transmitted in any form or by any means, including photocopying, recording, or other electronic or mechanical methods, without the prior written permission of the publisher, except in the case of brief quotations embodied in critical reviews and certain other noncommercial uses permitted by copyright law.

Every effort has been made to trace and seek permission for the use of the original source material used within this book. Where the attempt has been unsuccessful, the publisher would be pleased to hear from the author/publisher to rectify any omission.

First published in 2025 by Hambone Publishing
www.hambonepublishing.com.au

 A catalogue record for this book is available from the National Library of Australia

Editing by Mish Phillips and Jacki MacCullagh
Cover layout and illustrations by Jacki MacCullagh
Interior design by David W. Edelstein

For information about this title, contact:
Michael Meyer
michael@m31.com.au

ISBN 978-1-922357-91-5 (paperback)
ISBN 978-1-922357-92-2 (ebook)
ISBN 978-1-922357-93-9 (audiobook)

A Note of Gratitude

This book exists because of all the unique people who have walked beside me, pushed me forward, and occasionally smacked me over the head when I needed it.

To my wife, Anna: You are endlessly patient, wildly supportive, and somehow still here despite the ridiculousness I bring to the table.

To the quiet champions and behind-the-scenes mentors; you never asked for credit, but you damn well deserve it.

To the M31 team: You are the dreamers, the creatives, artistic doers, and the trusted advisors who make the impossible look easy and keep the wheels turning even when the road is pure chaos.

And to my family and friends, who embrace the unique, the direct, the sometimes chaotic, and the always-ours. I couldn't have asked for a better crew to keep me grounded while still nudging me toward the next big leap.

This one's for all of you and all the amazing people who see the world around them as though they can see The Matrix.

Now, let's get to it.

PRAISE FOR
WEIRD IS THE NEW NORMAL

I am delighted and enjoyed how Mike uses a mix of storytelling in the leadership lessons. The characters (Arcanus and the committee volunteers) and their adventures showed the importance of purposeful leading. It explains that leadership isn't about the activity but the outcome. This book taught me valuable ideas about leadership, making decisions, and creating real impact.

Jenalle Bushby — Canberra Branch Manager, Australian Computer Society (ACS)

It's been said that stories are always the shortest distance to the truth, and I think Mike has latched onto this. I've had a long journey both in leadership and storytelling, and I would say I have never come across the blend that Mike has managed in his book. It takes courage to mix the world of management and speak with the language of a fantasy story. It doesn't matter what our area of expertise is, we all surrender to the power of a well—told yarn and Mike's narrative draws you out on a pilgrimage full of surprises that indicate he's a man who has fixed on True North in his personal life.

Dr Paul Roe — The Outback Historian

When I received the transcript *Weird is the New Normal: The Unlikely Path of Leadership*, I anticipated a book from a highly qualified and technical professional aiming to share necessary leadership traits for today's complex and challenging organisational landscapes. I soon discovered that I was engaging with a richly layered work, guiding readers through a journey told in a charmingly mystical and quirky storytelling style, interwoven with established leadership traits and competencies framed for an emergent future.

I realised that this book also showcases Michael's remarkable gift for innovative thinking, highlighting his personal journey.

More importantly, it demonstrates how "Thinking Differently" can effectively challenge the leadership status quo and reshape our approach to leadership today, making it more relevant, responsive, and accountable to the emerging demands of modern and future organisational challenges. It emphasises that a successful "team" extends beyond the leader's contributions; rather, it encompasses the unique offerings of all individuals and how a leader successfully harnesses, develops, and nurtures this talent to achieve strong outcomes for the organisation, its members, and our shared world.

I recommend *Weird Is the New Normal: The Unlikely Path of Leadership* to all new or emerging leaders and current leaders who are challenged to think differently.

Nicholas Bewick — JP, FGIA, FCG (CS, CGP), FCPA, CA

Weird Is the New Normal: The Unlikely Path of Leadership is a bold and imaginative work that seamlessly intertwines professional insights with compelling storytelling. More than just a book, it's an immersive experience that challenges conventional leadership thinking while drawing readers into a richly crafted world.

What sets this piece apart is its ability to embed deep, practical lessons within an engaging fantasy narrative. Through the journey of Arcanus and his companions, readers explore themes like accountability, planning, and conflict resolution—lessons that apply as much to real—world leadership as they do to the characters' unfolding adventure. The balance of strategy, decision—making, and character—driven storytelling ensures that each chapter delivers both intrigue and insight.

For leaders, professionals, and lifelong learners, **Weird is the New Normal** offers a unique blend of wisdom and entertainment. It doesn't just teach leadership—it demonstrates it in action, making complex ideas more accessible and memorable. This is a must—read for those looking to grow, reflect, and be inspired. Highly recommended.

Shane Williams — Strategic Technology & Leadership Advisor

Sure, a family member might be expected to say nice things, but let's be honest: family also doesn't hold back when it comes to critique. If anything, they're often the toughest crowd.

That's why, as a school principal, I found myself captivated and inspired by this narrative, which blends fantasy with practical leadership insights. The shared principles resonated deeply with my own approach to leadership, reinforcing many strategies I already use and introducing new ideas to explore.

What truly surprised me, however, was the realisation that many of these leadership principles are equally vital for the teachers I lead in their classrooms. Clear communication, setting precise expectations, maintaining transparency, and demonstrating integrity are not only essential to effective leadership but also crucial in fostering an environment where both educators and students can thrive. By embodying these principles, we can minimise confusion, hesitation, and second—guessing, creating a stronger, more confident culture within our school.

Ella Meyer — Principal M.Ed., B.Ed., Adv.Dip.Counsel,MACE

Weird Is the New Normal: The Unlikely Path of Leadership is a captivating read, comprised of vibrant tapestry woven from threads of fantasy—fiction and practical leadership principles. Forget your dry business textbooks; this book invites you on a quest alongside Arcanus, a wizard whose journey to save his VUCA—a world that is riddled with challenges that mirror the complexities of modern management. Prepare to be transported to a realm where steam—powered water wheels become lessons in stakeholder value, and enchanted forests offer insights into strategic unity. This isn't just a story; it's a cleverly disguised masterclass in leadership, guaranteed to leave you both entertained and enlightened.

Beau Dean — MBA Student

"When your own father reviews your book, you brace for brutal honesty. Fortunately, he's a man who values a great story—and he found one here."

If you enjoy Matthew Reilly's action—packed style, this exciting and masterful storytelling tale will transport you to a dystopian universe of wizards and spells, leaving you spinning at the end and wanting more.

In this rollicking tale about Arcanus, his companions, and his enemies, Arcanus's leadership skills are tested and explored as each new challenge is encountered, and all is not as it seems.

This mysterious blend of wisdom and storytelling is engaging, entertaining, and informative. If you take the time to mine it well, this blend of wizardry and leadership will leave you with many new skills.

Dr Kenneth Meyer — Wired 4 Imagination

A Leadership Adventure Worth Taking — This book masterfully distils the wisdom of global leaders in business, leadership, and personal growth into a compelling and accessible guide. Rather than bogging readers down with heavy theory, it seamlessly weaves these lessons into the adventurous journey of Arcanus, a wizard on a quest to save his realm.

Through Arcanus' challenges and triumphs, the book illuminates the essential concepts that aspiring leaders must master. The storytelling approach makes the learning experience light, engaging, and easy to absorb. It's a refreshing alternative to traditional leadership books, offering practical insights without overwhelming the reader with dense frameworks.

I highly recommend this book to those embarking on their leadership journey. It won't drown you in abstract concepts but will equip you with the knowledge to seek deeper understanding. If you're looking for an enjoyable yet insightful read on leadership, this book is a fantastic choice.

Justeen Kirk — Founder & CEO

As an author, I deeply understand the passion and effort that goes into writing a book—it truly is a labour of love. In the moments I've had to read sections of *Weird is the New Normal*, I absolutely loved the concept. The storytelling is engaging and relatable and offers a fresh perspective that leaders can genuinely benefit from. I believe this approach will resonate with unique and diverse audiences, providing immense insight. I'm excited about the potential for this work to extend beyond the book format.

Katrina Macdermid — Cofounder & Director @ HIT Global

Mike Meyer's *Weird is the New Normal: The Unlikely Path of Leadership* is a refreshing take on leadership, blending elements of science fiction, fantasy, and tabletop role—playing games with real—world management strategies. As a neurodivergent IT professional turned business consultant, Meyer offers a unique perspective on leadership, making this book particularly valuable for those who don't fit the traditional corporate mould. By drawing parallels between workplace collaboration and adventuring parties, he highlights the importance of adaptability, strategic thinking, and teamwork in both fantasy and professional settings.

Through engaging storytelling, Meyer introduces characters like Berik, a resilient warrior and scout, and Arcanus, a visionary sorcerer, using their journey to illustrate different leadership styles and problem—solving approaches. His writing is both entertaining and practical, offering actionable advice while celebrating the strengths of diverse thinkers. With humour and insight, *Weird is the New Normal* encourages leaders to embrace creativity, inclusivity, and unconventional approaches, making it a compelling read for professionals, managers, and anyone navigating the challenges of the modern workplace.

Mike Parker — Founder @ Parker IT

Reading a situation is a leader's super power along with humility. Arcanus shows how these superpowers come together allowing him to recognise the needs of others and lead through empathy and empowerment. Unlike many other books about leadership, Michael has cleverly blended pop culture and theory to give practical examples of how to read between the lines to develop emotional intelligence and opportunities to reflect on Arcanus' experience to prepare the reader for their own leadership experiences. After all, leaders can be found at all levels of organisations and in society. Just like Arcanus, you don't need to be the strongest or most experienced, but you need to be committed to your quest. This book is excellent for those wishing to hone their skills at reading the situation and asking why.

Dr Vicki Gardiner — Associations Executive

In the current environment, where we face many challenges without an easy answer, all of us are on a quest that some days seems insurmountable. Michael's book is a lovely series of allegories through which some pretty hefty ideas are communicated in relation the often nuanced, contradicting and yet important concepts that make the difference between successfully leading people and just managing them. It encourages us to be authentic, to remember our values and to break our 'battles' into bite-sized chunks. This book will not be a once-read-only thing. It will be important to keep it close at hand for those hard days where some parts seem more relevant than others. On those days, it is a book to be used as a touchstone for reflection because some of the framework won't make any sense until you are in the middle of it!

Anneka Ferguson — Solicitor, Senior Lecturer, Amateur Adventurer and Philosopher, with a series of degrees (BALLB(Hons), GDLP, Grad.Dip Psych, M.IntLaw(Dist))

Navigation Guide

Chapter 0: The Skrol, The Staff, and The Unwritten Path.... 1

Chapter 1: A Journey Begun: A Leader's First Steps....... 23

Chapter 2: Echoes of the Elders, Wisdom, Water, and Wheels 41

Chapter 3: The Road Ahead – Trusting Instincts and Allies 65

Chapter 4: Gold, Greed, and the Bonds of Truth 91

Chapter 5: The Compass of Judicious Discernment.......119

Chapter 6: The Storm and the Calm..................... 153

Chapter 7: The Ledger and the Blueprint 183

Chapter 8: The Mantle of Trust and Counsel 219

Chapter 9: We're All Weird............................253

When This Book Isn't for You........................... 277

Chapter X: Waystones of Thought in the Librarians Hoard 281

Chapter XX: The Real Arcanus 287

CHAPTER 0

The Skrol, The Staff, and The Unwritten Path

Main Quest
The Odyssey of Purposeful Leadership

Arcanus awoke earlier than usual, his internal clock anxious to be off. After making a cup of elderberry tea, he went to sit by the window and stared out into the pale, grey-pink expanse. The city was a beautiful sight, quiet and peaceful, with ornately carved buildings and magnificent towers softly peeking out amongst the light mist. The City of Loria, vaunted for her magic and knowledge, was a sight to behold, especially for newcomers. The body of water surrounding the city centre gave it an ethereal quality, but more than that, it was one of the elements that powered wizards and mages. The natural elements, mountains, and magnificent forests created an unbelievable landscape that Arcanus knew he would remember for the rest of his life. He sighed as he looked at the candle sputtering low.

It was time. Time for him to set out on his quest. Though he had yearned for this day to arrive, he was nervous, judging by the sweat accumulating on his brow. His earlier years had prepared him for his journey to locate the Oracle, a mystical being known to have all the answers required to save his world, and yet, somehow, he was afraid he would fail. He was afraid he was not equipped with enough knowledge nor the skills required to pass through the quests each realm posed. He had been told he would find a "friend" or two to aid him, yet how does one deem someone new a friend or foe? How could he know they could be trusted, for his trust was not easily gained, especially over a short period of time?

His role as a specialist advisor often included advising kings and other leaders, guiding them through complex decisions and some ambiguous situations. It was his responsibility to solve problems and protect those who sought his counsel. His fellow wizards often spoke in hushed tones, trading theories about his place at the king's side. They sensed the trust bestowed upon him but could never quite grasp why—let alone how influence could flow without force, unseen yet unwavering. Arcanus was not comfortable taking the lead at this point in his life, and there was certainly no rush for him to step into that spot on a permanent basis. Anyone who understands leadership has been faced with this question: *Am I managing or leading?* And sometimes, it was difficult to answer. This assessment, a tough exam wizards went through on a yearly basis, was strange in some ways, and it was not the changes included but the way certain scenarios were posed.

As he reflected on his quest, Arcanus thought back to that very curious assessment completed several months ago. It was not just a refresher course, but more a record of growth (or lack thereof). He had always seen personal development as something without an end point, something which required constant working, dedication, and enthusiasm to be and do better. He never gave up and always made sure to view whatever conundrum faced him from a thousand and one angles. This adventure was something else though, he mused. Rather than taking on a specific individual, he had to prevent a catastrophe that had no boundaries, was faceless, and could consume all realms.

This got real all too soon, but Arcanus was confident he would find a way. That was his "why." Although young in age, his experience, raw talent, and never-say-die attitude were needed. His principles were deeply rooted, and he was known for providing his peers and those seeking his counsel the space to grow, to flourish, and to come into their own under his leadership and guidance. He valued their input, and this helped him hone his own abilities, especially when it came to crunch time—the all-important decision-making process. He had often seen others choke at this point, failing to pass and believing that was the sum of their value. By looking at it from a holistic viewpoint, he was able to find his place within any council and could point out weak spots that could affect a realm's ability to operate effectively. This made him a valuable asset within his realm, and beyond it. He would be starting out without a circle of influence, without a reassuring pat on the back or a letter offering him advice on next steps. He'd have to start from basics and keep a low profile as he made his way into the wide unknown. And that's where the entire affair started.

> "There are only two ways to influence human behaviour: you can manipulate it, or you can inspire it.
>
> Very few people or companies can clearly articulate why they do what they do. By why, I mean your purpose, cause or belief. Why does your company exist? Why do you get out of bed every morning? And why should anyone care?
>
> People do not buy what you do, they buy why you do it.
>
> We are drawn to leaders and organisations that are good at communicating what they believe. Their ability to make us feel like we belong, to make us feel special, safe and not alone, is part of what gives them the ability to inspire us."
>
> — Simon Sinek, Start With Why

Five years ago

Arcanus was born in the City of Loria fifteen years ago. Loria, a thriving hub of knowledge and power, was known for one thing—its Wizards and Mages. His parents recognised his affinity for magyck and knowledge, and instead of merely training him to be a warrior or common advisor, they explicitly chose to have him train at the Arcane Academy of Loria at the age of fifteen.

The Academy accepted only the best and brightest students, and Arcanus passed the entrance exams without difficulty.

It was there that he learned magyck sprang from two sources—light and dark—and that one could not exist without the other. While students were trained to understand both foundations, the Academy's mages deemed the practice of dark magic off-limits. His proficiency in basic spells and his specialisation in ancient magyckal texts and rune magycks earned him a hefty reputation, one he continually tried to shy away from. His assistance was sought out by fellow students and teachers alike, as his research skills and innovative spellcraft became widely known. This ensured that he was trained alongside the best warrior wizards, the first line of defence in their realm.

The future looked bright, and he was eager to learn.

And so, it continued—until everything changed.

Three months ago

It was maybe a quarter candle before dawn when Arcanus found a note slipped under his door. As a practicing wizard, he was given rooms at the Academy as long as he was teaching a class. Right now, he was teaching three, not counting his regular training.

A moon ago, he had come across an ancient Skrol, and for some reason, he was having great difficulty deciphering the text. He was learned in all common and uncommonly used tongues spoken by Wizards, Mages, and Humans, so this puzzled him beyond belief. That was red flag number one.

The second? The Skrol fairly reeked of something that made his skin crawl. He had shown it to the High Mage, and after prodding it open with the Staff of Khlus, a crystal staff powered by light itself (the High Mage had insisted on using it), his eyes flared with alarm as he backed away. He had asked Arcanus where he had found it, and, still unaware of the danger it contained, he had shrugged and told him.

The High Mage had immediately locked the Skrol away in a holy arca, a chest powered by the blessings of the highest elders, and told him to forget he had ever seen "the damned thing."

Arcanus had put it out of his mind—until the note was slipped under his door.

The Skrol of Caligo has been stolen.
All realms are in danger.
To find the answers you seek, search out The Lamia.
She will aid you in obtaining the Codex of Destiny.
Time is running out!

Of course, being a reasonable sort, he had immediately hightailed it to the High Mage and asked whether the Skrol was still safe. The Elder had turned several interesting shades of puce before sagging in his armchair and sadly shaking his head.

"You must find the Skrol, Arcanus. All our realms are in danger!"

Arcanus's brow furrowed. "I don't understand, Elder. What information does the Skrol hold?"

> "Living into our values means that we do more than profess our values; we practise them. We walk our talk. We are clear about what we believe and hold important, and we take care that our intentions, words, thoughts and behaviours align with those beliefs."
>
> — Brené Brown, Dare to Lead

> "If I really want to improve my situation, I can work on the one thing over which I have control—myself."
>
> — Stephen Covey, The 7 Habits of Highly Effective People

> "Let's make sure every last person on earth gets to do great work and be totally psyched while doing it."
>
> — Russ Laraway

> "Smile genuinely and make others feel important. People gravitate towards those who show genuine interest."
>
> — Dale Carnegie,
> How to Win Friends and Influence People in the Digital Age

> "How can NTs be so powerful? They are powerful because they are unified. They are unified because they are all the same. They are all the same because they conform. They conform because they are afraid to be different. They are afraid to be different because they might be ostracised. They might be ostracised because they are not powerful."
>
> — Ian Ford, A Field Guide to Earthlings

The High Mage took a deep breath, his expression grim. "The Skrol is a relic from an age long before ours, created by forces beyond our understanding. It holds knowledge and power that were never meant to be wielded by mortals. If it falls into the wrong hands, it could unravel the balance between light and dark itself."

Arcanus felt a chill run down his spine. "Then why was it left unguarded for so long?"

The Elder sighed. "Because for centuries, it was believed lost—hidden away by those who knew of its dangers. That it resurfaced now is no coincidence. Someone has been searching for it, and I fear it may be on the way to being delivered to them."

Arcanus's mind raced. He had always known magic came with responsibility, but this was something far greater. "Then we need to retrieve it before they do."

The High Mage nodded solemnly. "Indeed. That is why I am entrusting this task to you, you are resourceful, and you possess both the knowledge and the will to do what is necessary. The path ahead will not be easy, but if you fail—"

Arcanus hesitated, his mind racing for the right answer. "Elder, I have tried to be the greatest ambassador of our teachings—"

The Hight Mage interrupted "Yes, yes, all that, but what is it, the difference between you and every other wizard out there?"

Arcanus was silent as he stood thinking. After several moments of reflection, he straightened his posture and answered confidently. "I won't fail." Arcanus's voice was firm, even as uncertainty gnawed at the edges of his mind.

The High Mage responded quietly in a calming tone. "And

that is why you were selected above others. You seek no glory, yet you would give everything to see this quest succeed."

"You must take your leave before the city awakes. Tell no one of your mission. And take this."

Arcanus's eyes widened as the Elder handed him the Staff of Khlus.

"Elder, I cannot take this. You are the High Mage and greatest defender of our realm. This is yours to command."

The High Mage replied assuredly "When you come across the Skrol, and whoever holds it, chances are you will need to wield the staff to have any chance of saving our realms, Arcanus, talented as you are, without it, you have no chance. Best you seek out the Oracle to gain the information you need."

Arcanus replied in surprise "The Oracle? Isn't that a myth?"

The Elder studied him momentarily before placing a hand on his shoulder. "All myths start off with the truth; go forth and may the light guide your path."

With that, the quest had truly begun.

Meanwhile, in two different cities, a man and a woman have no idea they're destined to meet a brilliant wizard and possibly save the world.

Sorche stood staring at the note she'd received earlier. The staff for her sister's life, and if that wasn't bad enough, she'd already come across the powerful wizard before – when she stole the Skrol a few minutes after he'd left the High Elder's chambers. She sighed and rubbed her aching temples, wishing there was another way to get this done. She glanced back at the note – it seemed she had no choice but to comply.

In a different village, a warrior stood surveying the smouldering surroundings of his village. He roared at the Gods and promised vengeance would be his.

EDICTS OF THE WISE

Define Your Why or Someone Else Will

If you don't define your 'why,' someone else will define it for you.

Leadership isn't about waiting for permission—it's about choosing to step forward, even when no one asks you to.

The Cost of Avoiding Leadership

Refusing leadership doesn't mean avoiding responsibility—it just means giving up control over it.

If you don't take charge of the path ahead, someone else will, and you might not like where they lead.

The Adventure of Self-Discipline

This journey is about self-discipline.

The only thing we truly control is ourselves. Our actions. Our reactions. Our emotions. Nothing else is guaranteed. But if we master ourselves, we shape our own destiny.

Why does this matter? Because leadership, influence, and success start from within. If we don't have control over our own choices, how can we expect to guide others?

Leadership Shapes Who You Become

Who you are tomorrow depends on the choices you make today.

Leadership isn't just about decisions—it's about the kind of person those decisions turn you into.

Find Your Why, Build Your Mission

Knowing your why changes everything.

When you understand your purpose, you create a vision for where you're going. It gives direction. It builds motivation. It becomes a compass in chaos.

But it doesn't stop with you. A strong personal mission helps others find their own. When you understand your own drive, you can help others connect to theirs. That's where real influence happens. That's how leaders create lasting impact.

Motivation isn't something you force on people. It's something you awaken in them.

Connection Starts with Curiosity

A genuine smile sets the tone.

Whether in person or online, people respond to warmth. A simple smile, a kind word, or a thoughtful question builds trust.

People want to feel seen and valued. The best way to make that happen? Ask about them. Their story. Their perspective. Their challenges.

Curiosity isn't just about learning. It's about making people feel like they belong. When someone feels heard, they become part of the journey. And when people feel part of something, they give their best.

Navigating the Digital Age

The world has changed. What once felt normal now feels uncertain.

The digital age has broken old rules. It's full of nuance, complexity, and constant change.

Some people get lost in it. Others learn to see through it.

Those who can read between the lines—who see patterns in chaos, who understand the shifts beneath the surface—become leaders. They don't just survive this digital era. They master it.

Think of them as Captains on uncharted waters. They don't cling to old maps. They navigate, adapt, and take command.

The Hard Road is the Meaningful One

Leadership won't make life easier. It will make it more meaningful.

Easy paths lead to forgettable destinations. The best journeys demand effort, but they're the ones worth taking.

Your Greatest Tool is Reflection

As adventurers, leaders, and seekers, we often look outward for answers.

We search for tools, strategies, allies. But the greatest weapon and tool we have lies within.

Reflection and self-examination aren't weaknesses. They take courage. To stop. To look inward. To ask ourselves the hard questions.

Most people avoid this. It's uncomfortable. It forces us to confront our blind spots, our fears, our flaws. But true power comes from knowing yourself.

Know Yourself, Find Your Strength

When you understand your strengths, you use them better.

When you recognise your weaknesses, you can adjust.

When you discover your "why," you gain clarity. Purpose. Direction.

With this clarity, you can face anything. Ambiguity, failure, setbacks—they don't break you. They sharpen you.

The best leaders don't just charge forward. They know when to pause. When to reflect. When to refine.

Reflection isn't a retreat. It's an advance. A step toward becoming the kind of leader, the kind of adventurer, the world actually needs.

Influence Over Authority

You don't need a title to lead. You just need the courage to take responsibility.

Leaders aren't appointed. They are revealed through action.

Leadership is a Journey, Not a Title

Leadership isn't a destination. It's a path you walk every day.

If you think you've 'arrived,' you've already stopped leading.

Be Bold. Be Wise. Be You.

So, here's the challenge:

Be bold enough to know yourself.

Be wise enough to let that knowledge shape you.

Because the journey starts and ends with you.

Side Quest
Choosing the Right Steeds

Arcanus was making preparations for the quest ahead. As he ran through his checklist, he realised that he had not checked on a variable crucial to the journey – the horses!

Since he knew he would be traveling a great distance in search of the answers he sought, he required horses with good stamina, fit for endurance, and the ability to race away from trouble if and when it popped up. Seeing that this was his first time in charge of preparations, he had, unfortunately, underestimated their importance on the quest.

After speaking to the Academy stable master, Arcanus had asked him to recommend several horses for the journey. The stable master took him through the stables and the yards, and while the horses were well cared for, they were not suitable for endurance journeys as they had not been trained for such tasks.

Arcanus realised that while the stable master had taken the overall care of these beautiful creatures to heart and exercised great care towards his charges, he had not differentiated between the types of tasks the horses might be required to undertake at a moment's notice. That he had not done so was due to Arcanus not providing adequate instructions as he had recently been made the head of several minor departments, this being among them. He acknowledged the annoying truth to himself – that this would impact his upcoming journey, and after some reflection, took responsibility for not creating a clearer vision for the stable master.

Though Arcanus did not intend to squat on the man's head

and direct his every thought and movement from the neck down, there was such a thing as being too "hands off…" As someone who aspired to be the best version of himself, was he leading or simply managing the stable master? Surely there was a better way to accomplish this.

The stable master showed up the next morning and offered several suggestions. Arcanus evaluated each horse and found several aligned with his plan. The remaining horses, while beautiful, would not aid the journey. In fact, they'd probably add more time and possibly end up with more problems.

Arcanus asked the stable master about next steps, and the man revealed his idea to have the horses put through their paces; those which showed the most promise for a certain skill would be specifically trained in that field. That seemed a fine idea, and Arcanus let him know he thought so, taking care to express his approval of the man's enthusiasm and willingness to contribute. After the stable master ran him through the entire plan, Arcanus understood that he must also manage the stable master's expectations – this was a man who knew the Academy's horses like no other, and Arcanus respected his experience. It was important to tell him his experience and input were valued, and that he did a good job in translating Arcanus's vision and seeing the bigger picture. This was a learning curve for them both, and it taught Arcanus that his role as leader and manager were not one and the same, but two very separate skill sets that required him to turn his knowledge and ideas into action. Apparently, the stable master approved.

"I've seen things you wouldn't believe," the stable master said, absently running a hand over the mane of one of the chosen horses. "Strange things. Things that make a man question what he thinks he knows."

Arcanus raised an eyebrow. "You sound like you've been hanging around the old archives too long."

The stable master chuckled. "Maybe. Or maybe some mysteries are best left unsolved." He gave Arcanus a knowing look. "But for what it's worth... I want to believe."

Arcanus blinked, surprised at the turn in the conversation. A slow grin crept across his face. "Well, keep your eyes open. The truth is out there."

The stable master frowned. "Where?"

> *"Trying is the first step towards failure."*
> *"Failure delivers the opportunity to learn and grow by doing. "*
> – Homer Simpson, The Simpsons S9 Ep9

Side Quest
Wisdom in the Stables

The stable master was looking at Arcanus for direction, and he found himself facing a bit of a quandary: How could they ensure that each special group maintained its strengths at all times?

He needed to bounce ideas off someone, and who better than the High Elder—someone he not only admired but respected?

The High Elder was fond of his visits, especially as they provided an opportunity to see Arcanus, his star pupil, express his thoughts on various subjects. Today, however, Arcanus had come with a specific concern.

He sat down with the High Elder, and after making small talk for several minutes, he brought up the issue concerning the stable master, how the problem had come about, and the ideas they had come up with to solve it.

The High Elder applauded Arcanus for taking responsibility and accountability for his actions and accepting the consequences thereof. He suggested consulting with one of the city's best equestrians, a woman known far and wide for her skills in working with horses of all shapes and sizes. Arcanus agreed readily, hoping to obtain relevant advice that would fit his plan.

The Next Day

Arcanus met the equestrian expert, Lilia, and found her pleasant and knowledgeable. She understood his dilemma and offered her farm as a training ground where she would take over and implement a tried-and-tested strategy.

He thought about this for a moment. While the opportunity would allow him access to one of the best and brightest—a leader in her own right—it wasn't a solution that aligned with the plan he and the stable master had created. He also didn't want to farm the work out to another.

After thanking her for the offer, he explained the plan and the steps they had taken. She seemed impressed that he had the confidence not only to decline her offer but also to articulate the idea, acknowledge the obstacles he and the stable master had encountered, and think out loud about ways to push through them.

Lilia provided several tips that aligned with his vision of upgrading the in-house training curriculum. She advised him to scribe great ideas down—something he already did regularly for other events. She suggested discussing these ideas with a trusted friend or colleague, in this case, the stable master, as he understood the *why* behind the tasks and could help Arcanus remain focused on attaining his goals. Finally, she emphasised reviewing notes regularly to keep track of progress.

Arcanus thanked her for her time and valuable advice, and she regarded him for a moment before saying,

"Arcanus, you are a bright and talented individual with foresight beyond your years. Confidence without arrogance, respect for others, and a willingness to reflect on yourself and grow from that reflection means you are finally there—ready to step out of others' shadows and become a leader in your own right. I would be happy to stand as a sounding board for your ideas, should you need one. Leaders need good advisors, and I offer my counsel willingly."

Humbled by her praise, Arcanus accepted her offer. She smiled.

"If we fail to anticipate the unforeseen or expect the unexpected in a universe of infinite possibilities, we may find ourselves at the mercy of anyone or anything that cannot be programmed, categorised, or easily referenced."

Arcanus broke into a huge smile and replied, "Do you think I'm Spooky?"

She tilted her head for a moment, trying to make sense of his quip, then winked.

It had been a fulfilling and exciting day. Arcanus had set out seeking an expert but ultimately realised he hadn't truly been looking for help—rather, for someone to bounce ideas off of. With a smile, he departed with easy steps, confident that he had this well in hand.

THE UNWRITTEN RULES

Silence isn't empty—it's useful

People rush to fill silence, but real leaders know when to hold it. A pause can mean someone is thinking, processing, or just being comfortable. Let silence do its work. It reveals what's beneath the surface, gives space for real insight, and keeps you from speaking just to be heard.

Follow-up isn't extra work—it's leadership

Following up after a meeting doesn't just show you care—it shows you're paying attention. Checking in helps you see past surface-level responses, dig into what really matters, and align actions to outcomes. Small follow-ups build big trust.

Your reputation enters the room before you do

People decide who you are before you even speak. How you show up, handle pressure, and treat others writes your reputation long before you introduce yourself. Guard it, because the effort to overcome it is higher once it's damaged.

You teach people how to treat you

What you allow is what continues. Set weak boundaries? Expect people to push them. Overcommit? People will keep piling on. Act with integrity? You'll get respect. Every interaction trains people on what to expect from you—make sure you're setting the right standard.

THE MIRROR OF MASTERY

» What drives you to get up every day and contribute to something bigger than yourself?

» How does your unique role within your current adventure shape the impact you have on others?

» If you could design your ultimate adventure, what would it look like, and how would it inspire others?

CHAPTER 1

A Journey Begun: A Leader's First Steps

Main Quest
The Odyssey of Purposeful Leadership

Arcanus adjusted the straps on his pack and took a deep breath. He had left before the city awoke, just as the High Mage had instructed, and now he found himself on the open road, bound for lands he had only read about in ancient texts. As he'd saddled his steed and an accompanying horse that morning, he was thankful that the stable master had found him horses trained for endurance and fleet of foot. With the light of dawn on his back, he set out.

The morning air was crisp, carrying with it the scent of damp earth and pine. His horse moved at a steady pace, hooves clopping rhythmically against the dirt path. He had spent years preparing for this moment—studying magyck, honing his skills, learning the histories of the realms—but none of that quite prepared him for the weight of responsibility now resting on his shoulders.

He reached into his satchel, fingers brushing over the Staff of Khlus, the weight of it reassuring. It was both a weapon and a key, a piece of history entrusted to him with a purpose he was still trying to fully grasp.

The road stretched ahead, winding through dense forests and over rolling hills. He knew this was only the beginning. The real challenge lay beyond the horizon, in whatever dangers awaited him.

He had a feeling that his life was about to change, though how, he knew not. The scenery was so familiar to him, almost beloved in a way, and yet he had a gnawing feeling that he wouldn't look at it the same way again. He told himself it was just his imagination running wild, and that once he had completed this quest, he'd return home, hopefully with more experience and a certain amount of wisdom under his belt. Time would tell.

With a final glance back toward the city he called home, Arcanus spurred his horse forward. The adventure had begun.

He rode hard for several hours until he came to a familiar sight, a small village with a large river. A few minutes later, he spied The Fat Duck Inn. He headed for the inn's stables where he cursed himself for being all kinds of foolish. He should have brought a companion, someone who could look after the horses and supplies.

"So eager to save the world, yet I forget to bring the most basic help needed to ensure my traveling companions are well cared for... Yup, I'm a dumbass."

He had to make right the problem, and after a moment, he located a lad eager to earn a few coins.

"You, boy, do you know anything about horses?"

The lad nodded and shyly told Arcanus his father had a farm where he was in charge of seeing to the horses' care. Pleased, Arcanus realised the boy already had some prior knowledge. All he had to do was set him up for success – that meant providing clear instructions, letting him feel like he could ask questions if he was unsure, and making sure he felt confident in his method of care. Of course, the payment due to him when Arcanus set out next was an incentive, but he could see the lad was eager to please, and a few words of approval would boost his confidence.

Arcanus told him to provide each horse with a double groom, that they needed to be blanketed, and fed a double measure of oats along with their regular feed. As they got to chatting, Arcanus watched the lad work and noticed he was a tad nervous.

"Calm down, lad. Your nervous behaviour will make the horses nervous. Care to mention what ails you?"

"I wants to do a good job, sir, but I ain't never looked after 'orses this foine afore."

Arcanus understood – the boy was afraid of messing up, and it was his job to set him straight. The lad's gaze was fixed straight ahead, and Arcanus knew he had to connect with him if he had any chance of setting him at ease.

"You've done a wonderful job so far and followed all instructions to the letter."

The boy looked up and caught Arcanus's gaze with a look of delight.

"Really?!" he said, forgetting his nerves for the moment.

"Truly. I'm confident I've left the horses in good hands. Remember, if you have any questions, just ask or inform the innkeeper that you need to speak to me."

The boy nodded and went back to his work, standing taller and looking more confident. It does not take much to show people you care, Arcanus realised, and it could make a world of difference to them.

> *"The single most important thing a manager can do is help their people achieve their short term and long-term career aspirations."*

A JOURNEY BEGUN: A LEADER'S FIRST STEPS

> *"Managers are failing, and no one is helping. We do not need another person's opinion about what it means to be a great manager; we need to learn to lead in a way that delivers more engaged employees and better business results."*
>
> — Russ Laraway, When They Win, You Win

Arcanus headed for the inn and sat himself down to a well-earned tankard of ale and a bowl of stew, asking the innkeeper, Jameson, to send some food out for the new stable boy. He had known Jameson for several years and had helped him out with a serious issue the year before. He knew he could rely on him for discretion and information.

The inn was busy at this time of day and paying little attention to the loud chatter around him, Arcanus tucked into the simple food with relish. After several minutes, he saw Jameson heading his way with two tankards of ale.

The innkeeper nodded as he sat down, taking a hearty sip before leaning in and speaking in a low tone.

"Ye remember what ye did for the village last year? The same thieving blighters are back, threatening us, burning crops and for what? Lookin' for some woman carryin' a magical stick…"

Arcanus's ears perked up at the mention of a woman with information.

"What woman?"

"They're looking for someone called 'the informer.' Apparently, she stole somethin' of value from some fancy folk up North, and the Lord who funds these hooligans wants it."

A realisation struck him—this informer had to be the one who had stolen the Skrol. And if she had it, she would soon be coming for the Staff of Khlus as well.

All he had to do was lay his trap and wait.
"Is she in the village?"

> "When we feel safe among the people with whom we work, we are more likely to survive and thrive."
>
> "Great leaders truly care about those they are privileged to lead and understand that the true cost of the leadership privilege comes at the expense of self-interest."
>
> — Simon Sinek, Leaders Eat Last

> "True leadership is not about control but about enabling others to thrive."
>
> — The Trusted Advisor

Sorche's head ached as she blinked her eyes. She'd consumed too much ale the night before, trying to ply information out of these simpletons. Just as she was about to throw in the towel, she'd heard that a wizard was on his way, a friend of the villagers apparently, and someone who brought them good fortune. It seemed like her luck had finally turned.

She stretched and rubbed a grimy hand across her face, trying to stifle a yawn that was wide enough to split her face in two. She needed a bath and some food before she set out hunting for the man who held the key to her sister's freedom.

Sorche thought back to several months ago. Her trade was in secrets and much as she tried to keep her family out of her life, dangerous as it was, sometimes, an enemy put two and two together and came up with Emilé – her beloved sister.

Sorche had been hired to discover a relic of great value, and somewhere along the journey, she'd had a change of heart. Discovering that her employer was a no-good piece of shyte (who thought he could somehow bring about the end of the world with a piece of parchment and a magyckal stick), Sorche started digging for information. What she found did not ease her mind whatsoever, and she felt that she'd firmly landed arse overhead.

Her employer was someone skilled in magycks and he did intend to bring about the end of the known world. After laughing hysterically for a minute, Sorche wondered what to do: play along and once she'd got hold of the relics, destroy them, or return the coin she was paid in advance and decline the trip. The latter might land her in all sorts of shyte, and she'd never been one to shy away from a good challenge. After several months of searching, plying eager mouths with ale, and listening to gossip, she'd finally learned the Skrol's location.

Unfortunately for her, once she'd stolen that piece of parchment, the hounds of hell set upon her, and she was barely a step or two ahead of them at every turn. It was too dangerous to try and steal the staff from the old man at the academy, now that they were all on guard, so she set a trap. She paid a messenger to leave a note under the young wizard's door. Since he was the one who discovered the parchment and seeing that he was such a goody two shoes, no doubt he'd come after the Skrol.

What Arcanus didn't know was that the informer had paid the messenger to deliver two messages, the second to the old man informing him of the stakes.

She rolled out of bed and after a quick series of warm up exercises that got her blood flowing, she requested the morning meal in her room. The Fat Duck had simple fare, but it was decent enough to stave off her hunger for the moment. By all accounts, she should have the staff in her possession today. The main problem was how to get it?

EDICTS OF THE WISE

Your Success is Measured by Your Team's Results

Your impact as a leader isn't just about what you achieve—it's about the results your team delivers. You don't win alone. Your success comes from guiding, influencing, and supporting others. If you want your team to create amazing results, you need to set them up to win.

Give Them a Clear Mission and Vision

Big or small, every team needs a purpose. Create a vision and mission that everyone can get behind. Don't just dictate it—let the team contribute. When people help shape the mission, they take ownership of it. Show them how their work connects to a bigger picture.

People aren't just motivated by money. They want to contribute to something meaningful. They want their work to matter. Make sure they see the value in what they do. When people feel like their contributions make a difference, they perform at their best.

Be Real, Be Genuine, and Actually Care

If you want a strong team, get to know your people. Understand what drives them, what excites them, and what they care about. Work with them, not just above them. Celebrate their contributions. And don't fake it.

People can spot fake leadership a mile away. A leader who pretends to care is worse than one who doesn't care at all. Be authentic. Be present. If you truly value your team, they will go above and beyond for you.

Trust Them to Do Their Job

Trust, trust, trust. That's the foundation of leadership. Your job isn't to do the work for them—it's to set expectations, provide guidance, and then step back.

Let them execute. Let them deliver. Don't fall into the trap of thinking only you can do the job right. That's arrogance, not leadership. Give them space to succeed—and to fail.

Work Without Purpose is Just Motion

Busy doesn't mean productive. Leadership isn't about keeping people occupied—it's about making sure their time is spent creating impact. A team that's working hard but not delivering value is just running in circles. Leadership cuts through the noise and focuses on what actually moves the needle.

Feedback Should Be Constant and Useful

Feedback isn't a once-a-year thing. It should happen daily. Make it part of normal conversations. Keep it clear, keep it helpful, and make it two-way. If something needs to be improved, address it. If something is going well, acknowledge it.

And for the love of leadership—DO NOT use the "criticism sandwich." That tired old formula of praise, criticism, praise doesn't work. It just confuses people. Be direct, be constructive, and make sure feedback leads to action.

Coach, Mentor, and Grow Your Team

Great leaders don't just manage—they develop people. Be available. Coach them. Mentor them. Help them grow into the best version of themselves. Teach them how to think critically, how to problem-solve, and how to lead.

A strong team isn't built overnight. Invest in them. If you want long-term results, you need long-term development.

Let Them Succeed and Fail on Their Own

Your team needs to win and lose on their own merit. That's how they grow. Your role isn't to prevent failure—it's to guide them through it. Set clear expectations, then step back and let them own their work.

Chase excellence, not perfection. Perfection is a distraction. Get the details right where they matter, but don't get lost in the weeds. Use the technical and deep granular insights to your advantage as a group and focus on the 20/80 rule—20% of the high-priority work delivers 80% of the impact. Prioritise smartly.

Your Standards Set the Bar

The level you accept is the level your team will perform at. If you allow sloppy work, weak accountability, or a lack of ownership, don't be surprised when that becomes the norm.

Set the bar high. Hold yourself and your team to a standard of clarity, excellence, and accountability. What you allow is what you'll get.

Invest in Career Conversations

People don't just want jobs—they want growth. Have career conversations. Ask them where they want to go. Help them build the skills they need to get there. Align their growth with the team's goals.

Be strategic. Help them plan for the future. A leader who supports career development creates a team that performs better, stays longer, and appreciates the investment. And when they do leave? They'll leave as an advocate for your leadership.

Play to Strengths—Put People Where They Can Win

Great teams aren't built by making everyone the same. They're built by understanding individual strengths and putting people where they can thrive. Leadership isn't about forcing people into roles that don't fit—it's about positioning them to succeed. If someone is struggling, don't assume they're the problem—maybe they're just in the wrong role. Know your people. Set them up for success. Let them run.

Remove Roadblocks—That's Half the Job

A leader's job isn't just to set direction—it's to clear obstacles so the team can move forward. If your people are stuck in process hell, blocked by red tape, or fighting uphill battles, that's on you. Leadership isn't just directing —removing friction, fighting for resources, and ensuring your team has what they need to win. When in doubt, ask yourself: Am I helping, or am I in their way?

Resilience Separates Good Leaders from Great Ones

Resilience comes from knowing how to handle pressure, manage emotions, and guide others through challenges. It's okay to feel things—but it's not okay to let those emotions take control. Leaders who stay steady in tough situations keep teams focused, motivated, and moving forward.

Setbacks will happen. The difference between an average leader and a great one is how they handle those setbacks. Some leaders panic, blame others, or retreat into fear-based decision-making. The best leaders stay steady, adjust, and lead with confidence. They know how to reframe setbacks as learning moments, push ahead without burning out, and keep trust intact even when things get hard.

GO AND LEARN EQ.

Side Quest
Stuck in the Mud

Two years ago

The morning sun painted the jagged peaks in gold as the party left the Fat Duck Inn behind, the air crisp with the promise of adventure. Ahead, the mountain pass narrowed sharply, its rocky trail a challenge for any traveller. As they rounded a bend, the sound of shouting caught their attention. A group of traders surrounded a heavily laden cart, its wheels sunk deep into the muddy trail.

Arcanus raised his hand for silence. "What's going on here?"

A burly man, clearly the leader, threw up his hands. "I'm Nate, this cart's stuck, and the driver can't get it moving. I've been trying to get them to hurry it along, but nothing's working."

A young lad helping the traders folded his arms. "And by 'hurry it along,' you mean?"

"Shouting instructions," the man admitted, scowling.

The team pulling the cart, for they had no horses or oxen, grunted and mumbled beneath their breath. A wiry young woman known as Ruby, clearly the one directing the cart rolled her eyes. "He's been telling me to push this, pull that, move here, go there, but the problem's the load and the wheels. I've been trying to explain that, but he won't listen…"

Arcanus stepped forward. "Nate, you're micromanaging. That's not leadership—it's interference. Let your driver do their job."

The trader bristled. "And what am I supposed to do, just stand here?"

Arcanus interjected, his tone steady. "No, you lead. Start with feedback. Be clear, be candid, and be connected. Ask her what's wrong, listen to her expertise, and then help her succeed."

Arcanus gestured toward the cart. "And while you're at it, set your team up for success. Lighten the load if you can, clear the path, and make sure she has what she needs. Your role is to remove obstacles, not create them…"

Nate frowned, then nodded slowly. "Alright Ruby, what do you need?" he asked the driver.

Ruby grinned. "Can you help unload some of the crates and clear those rocks ahead."

As the team worked together, the cart began to move, the wheels breaking free from the mud. When the cart finally rolled forward, the trader approached Arcanus, patting the back of his shoulders. "Didn't realise I was the one holding us back. Thanks for showing me the way."

Arcanus smiled faintly. "Leadership isn't about doing everything yourself. It's about empowering others to succeed. When they win, you win."

Arcanus grinned, glancing at the cart as it trundled away. "Or, as a certain Time Lord once said, 'You don't just fix things. You make them better.'"

Nate looked at Arcanus with a puzzling expression. "Time Lord?"

Arcanus waved him off with a grin. "Just someone who's seen enough to know a little wisdom goes a long way."

As the party continued their climb through the pass, Nate grunted. "A Time Lord, huh? Are we going to run into one next?"

Arcanus grinned, waving his robe around him with a flourish. "You never know, boys. But if we do, I'm always ready to learn something new."

> "In 900 years of time and space,
> I have never met anyone who was not important."
> — Doctor Who, Season 6, Episode 0: A Christmas Carol

Side Quest
The Architect and the Veteran

The ancient stone bridge arched gracefully over a wide, rushing river, its weathered surface etched with centuries of footsteps and wagon wheels. As Arcanus' party approached, they noticed a small group gathered near the middle of the bridge. A young knight in polished armour stood stiffly, holding a scroll, while a grizzled commander frowned deeply, his arms crossed. The air crackled with tension.

"Another dispute," Bailey muttered as they neared. "Looks like we're not getting across this bridge without stepping into it."

Arcanus nodded. "Go ahead, Bails. This one feels like it's in within your wheelhouse."

Bailey nodded and approached, "What's going on here?"

The knight glanced nervously at the commander, then spoke. "I've been tasked with overseeing the upgrades to the bridge. It needs reinforcing to support heavier traffic. But the commander doesn't agree with my plan."

"It's reckless," the commander growled. "He wants to

tear out the old stones entirely. This bridge has stood for generations."

Bailey raised an eyebrow, looking between them. "Both of you want the same thing—a bridge that stands and serves the kingdom. So, what's really the issue here?"

The knight hesitated. "I—I don't think he trusts my decisions. He's been in charge of this region for years, but I'm just starting out. If I mess up, it's on me."

The commander scoffed. "It's not about trust. It's about strategy. He's not thinking long-term."

Bailey folded his arms. "Sounds to me like you both need to help each other. Commander, when was the last time you coached him on handling a project like this?"

The commander frowned, taken aback. "I... well, I haven't."

Bailey turned to the knight. "And you—have you asked for his advice? Or are you trying to prove yourself without help?"

The knight looked down at the scroll in his hands. "I guess I thought I needed to figure it out on my own."

Bailey nodded, pleased they'd come to these conclusions so readily. "Here's what you'll do. Commander, share your knowledge. Not just about bridges but about leading that promotes thinking long-term. And you," he said, pointing to the knight, "listen. Ask questions. Let him guide you—but don't lose sight of your role. You're leading this, and that means you take ownership."

The commander crossed his arms. "And if I don't agree with his final decision?"

"Then you coach him through the consequences," said Bailey. "You're not here to make his choices—you're here to make him better at making them."

The knight looked up, his eyes brightening. "And if I succeed, it's because I had your help."

The commander's face softened. "Fine. We'll do it your way. But I'll be watching."

Bailey muttered a silent prayer and smiled faintly. "Good. A strong leader makes their people better, not by doing the work for them, but by helping them grow."

As the group began discussing the bridge's future, one of the villagers nearby approached Bailey. "You sound like you've done this before."

Bailey chuckled and waved at the group of wizards. "Sometimes, the best thing you can build isn't a bridge—it's a person. We've all been through this." Then, with a smirk, he added, "As a wise alchemist once said, *'It's not an experiment if you know it's going to work.'*"

The villager frowned. "An alchemist?"

Bailey waved a hand. "Never mind. Just remember: when they are winning, you'll know."

The party crossed the bridge as the sun dipped lower, leaving the knight and commander to their work, both now building something far more enduring than stone.

THE UNWRITTEN RULES

Acknowledge Before You Act—But Keep It Natural

Jumping straight into a task without a greeting can come across as cold, but forced small talk isn't the answer either. Keep it simple and authentic. A quick "Hey, hope your day is going well" or "Morning!" is enough. Acknowledge, but don't overthink it.

Respect Time—Yours and Theirs
(Even If Time Management Is Hard)

Time blindness is real, but that's not an excuse. Set alarms, use calendar reminders, and give yourself buffers if you struggle with punctuality. If you're late, let people know. If you're running a meeting, stick to the agenda so it doesn't drag on. Respecting time is respecting each other.

Conversations Are a Two-Way Street—Use Structured Engagement

Social interactions can feel overwhelming or unstructured. The trick? Follow a simple pattern: Listen, acknowledge, respond, return the conversation. If someone shares something, respond in a way that connects but then shift the focus back to them (e.g., "That sounds great! I also enjoy that—what got you into it?"). Or share your story and then link it back to what was said. This prevents overtly info-dumping or unintentional one-sided conversations.

Engage with Intent—Find Your Own Way to Stay Present

Not everyone can sit still and focus the same way. Eye contact isn't required—use other ways to show you're engaged, like nodding, summarising their point, or asking follow-up questions. If staying still is difficult, doodle, fidget, or take notes—whatever helps you stay tuned in. Presence isn't about looking engaged—it's about actually engaging.

THE MIRROR OF MASTERY

» How can I ensure that my feedback focuses on behaviours and outcomes without unintentionally sounding critical of the person?

» Am I creating an environment where my team feels safe to express their thoughts and mistakes without fear of judgment?

» Do I balance directness with empathy, and how can I develop a consistent approach to showing I care personally?

CHAPTER 2

Echoes of the Elders, Wisdom, Water, and Wheels

Main Quest
The Odyssey of Purposeful Leadership

It was a fine morning, and the mist that had settled overnight slowly cleared, leaving the village with crisp, clean air. The past few weeks had turned up naught on the informer, and truth be told, Arcanus was becoming a tad frustrated.

He had paid messengers who travelled ahead of him, sending back news, updates, false leads, and more. It was a trying time, but thankfully, on his last day there, he finally obtained a nugget of information as to her whereabouts. Looking out the window, he could see the steam-powered water wheel pumping the precious, life-giving fluid throughout the village, and thought back to the day they had decided to install it. More than that, he thought about the lessons he had learned. He was older than most could imagine, but it was never too late to pick up a pearl of wisdom.

Three Weeks Ago

Arcanus had been in Elipa for a few days when their well ran dry. The village "sorcerer" hadn't managed to divine a new water source close to the village, and the villagers were fed up. Seeing a few threaten the man, Arcanus decided to step in and see how he could help. He was not a fan of conflict and preferred working through things in a logical manner. This was not everyone's cup of tea, but short of clubbing the man over the head for being a fraud, that wouldn't solve the issue currently facing them: no water.

Berik, a man of few words and a capable warrior-turned-smithy, was passing through the village when he spied the altercation. Arcanus had met Berik a few years ago, and he had become a good friend. After hearing about the village's quandary, he volunteered to help them figure out a way to drive water up the steep incline and into the village.

Arcanus, Lukas the Innkeep, Taylor the Smithy, and Berik drew up some plans with various possible solutions. Unfortunately, and just their luck, several elders overheard them and wandered over. Arcanus groaned inwardly—elders more often than not provided nothing but cheeky opinions. They apparently refused to leave such an important task to the "younglings," and after arguing all the pros and cons for each idea, they started arguing amongst themselves.

It didn't matter to them that no one fully understood any of the ideas they had been reading about. What mattered to them was the responsibility of the task and who would oversee it. Sure, a foreman was important, but if one did not have a project to lead, did it matter that they were a foreman?

Arcanus was about to raise his voice when one of the elders hit him hard across the back with their walking stick.

"Hey! That hurt!"

The elder smirked and chuckled.

"Don't think I don't see you, young whippersnapper!"

"Elder, I meant no disrespect, but this isn't something that requires a committee..."

Arcanus could feel their united glare almost set fire to his ensemble, and that was not something he wanted, as he was wearing his favourite set of purple robes gifted to him by the High Elder. Lost in thought for a second, he felt a sharp SWISH! knock his wizard's hat off.

"Sir, I take offense to the harm aimed at my ensemble!"

The elders cackled in toothless unison as he mumbled under his breath about "no respect," then dusted off and set his precious hat back on his head.

"What would you know about leading via a committee, young man?"

He met a shrewish pair of eyes peering at him, almost like he was an irritating fly caught in the grips of the dreaded demon of fire and darkness. He was ashamed to admit it, but he believed he almost pantsed himself at that moment.

"I am several decades older than you, Elder... I'm just blessed with eternally youthful looks, like the halflings in the next shire..."

"Don't you sass me, young man! You're not so old that I cannot paddle your backside!"

Bollocks! Surely, he was not in the midst of a shouting match with someone who had barely looked at the plans but was now disagreeing over them?!

"Err, of course not, Elder. I await your feedback."

He excused himself and headed back to Berik and Lukas, rolling his eyes at both. They, of course, did not commiserate and had a hard time keeping their grins in check. After several hours, Gregori the Wise, leader of the elder committee, stopped and tapped Arcanus on the shoulder.

"We have agreed that a steam-powered water wheel is the most valuable and efficient option..."

Arcanus closed his eyes to stop himself from rolling them yet again, lest they get stuck back there. He, Lukas, and Berik had decided this was the best solution hours ago...

He nodded and thanked Gregori, watching him shuffle back to their table.

Berik snorted and rubbed his eyes, mumbling that the

elders had robbed him of his will to live. Lukas chuckled, explaining why the elders wanted to be involved.

"See here, lad. They were once the strongest o' the village, and everyone looked t' them for assistance. As they grew older and frailer, they were seen as wise members from the old days, but their frailty somehow gave the impression that it interfered with their ability to get things sorted out, so the villagers stopped consulting 'em altogether. Ye ken, if one has no sense of purpose or value, it impacts ye in more ways than one."

That was something Arcanus could understand. They wanted to be seen, heard, and appreciated for their input.

As a wizard, it would have been fairly easy for him to rig a spell and get the new water source done that way; however, he was looking to bolster the villagers' spirits, have them put forth a solution, and contribute to the build—contribute to something of great value to everyone here. He knew many were capable workers and wanted to see what they could do when put to the task. As someone familiar with village squabbles and how they usually required a mediator—aka the village elders—to decide who was right, he knew this might be a tricky task, especially after it had taken them hours to decide on a path forward.

> *"The quest for value must be a lifelong passion that you pursue with single minded focus."*
>
> *"As a leader, you are not there to simply be a personal role model. You are there to create value."*
>
> *"No matter how you define it, you need to understand that the only reason your organisation exists in the first place is to create value for its stakeholders."*
>
> — Martin G. Moore, No Bullsh!t Leadership

That had been a fine three weeks of hard work, and what's more, several young men had found their passion and purpose in life—a real sense of meaning and value they hadn't known before. Arcanus knew internal motivation, had experienced it himself, and this was something none of them would ever forget. They were part of the village and now understood what it meant to serve their people and the value that service provided.

While studying for leadership quests at the academy, the tutors often asked them to question themselves: As leaders, what's in it for you? Why are you whipping up a spell to make natural jellied fruits one can simply pluck from trees and stew down? What do you hope to get out of such an invention or idea?

This might seem like a self-serving question, but for someone like Arcanus, who constantly sought ways to improve himself and grow through experience, this would help him move past the regular nonsense that would bog them down like a constipated fishwife! He had never been someone motivated by money or other material things; rather, he had found value in positive results. In his mind, it was the only real way to measure one's progress.

"Ah, Arcanus, what brings you back?"

A heavy hand jolted him out of his memories, and he coughed hard, trying not to vomit up the second mug of ale he had been enjoying. Berik certainly had a hard way of greeting his friends—literally.

"Greetings, Berik! Good to see you again. How are things at home?"

"Tough. Since we last met, raiders burnt down most of my village… I, I lost my family."

Arcanus nodded sorrowfully and glanced at his friend's

tense, angry face. He could feel the weight of responsibility on Berik's shoulders. The man was quiet, someone who didn't waste words. When he spoke, it was always in measured tones.

Arcanus opened his mouth to offer words of comfort, but Berik held up a hand.

"I don't feel that I can speak of it yet. Please, no questions or condolences now."

Arcanus nodded, having no wish to intrude upon the man's thoughts. He turned back to Lukas and asked whether he had heard anything more about new travellers passing through the village.

"Hmm, no one aside from the lassie upstairs."

His ears perked up. A new traveller—and a woman at that.

Feigning a casual interest, he tried to pry more information out of Lukas. He had known Lukas for a while, but some days, the man simply couldn't focus on one topic of conversation, and right now, he was more interested in setting up a local competition, the "Bru Ha Ha" for the best brew.

"Lukas! What do you know about her?"

Lukas scratched his chin, annoyed to have his attention diverted from talking about his newest ale.

"I'll tell ye what I know IF ye promise te help me set up a machine so I can refine the ale. It's a good ale, but I believe it can be better. I've been makin' small changes over time and loggin' the results so I know what I want to make, but I need someone able to craft fine, err, non-human tools I can use te perfect it."

Arcanus chuckled and shook his head. "You know I cannot help you cheat, Lukas."

"Nae, it's no' cheating! I am making the ale meself. I just need the proper equipment, and I have already drawn it out, so this is comin' from my mind, ye ken?"

> "I define a leader as anyone who takes responsibility for finding the potential in people and processes, and who has the courage to develop that potential."
>
> — Brené Brown, Dare to Lead

> "Your job is not to do the work yourself, but to guide your team to the best possible outcome."
>
> — Kim Scott, Radical Candor

Upstairs

Sorche knew the staff carrier was staying at The Fat Duck. She'd already searched his room, the stables and the surrounding area, unsuccessfully and now wondered where he'd stored it. She had also found out he had made enquiries after her. They'd been in the same common room several times, but she'd been wary and stayed under the radar. She had to tread carefully, else her plan to save her sister would fail. Blast Rafe, and his psychotic desires! Not much was known about the dark wizard, save that he was old, powerful, hadn't been seen in decades, and had been searching high and low for several ancient objects of great power.

She thought for several minutes and decided she might have better luck on the road, perhaps catch him unawares. Flinging her belongs into the small knapsack, she eased her way down the stairs and after checking her surroundings, quietly exited the Inn and set off to lie in wait several miles down the road. She knew the wizard's travel plans, not that it was difficult to guess as he could only go in one of two directions, toward Loria or away.

Sorche was so busy thinking ahead that she didn't pay attention to the road, and several hours later found herself surrounded from all sides by a group of rebels. Cursing to herself, she dismounted, taking care not to draw attention to her knapsack.

Unfortunately, rebels being what they are, were always in need of gold and other supplies, and they snatched the pack from her. Dumping the contents on the ground, they came across a letter with Rafe's seal. Recognising the value of their prisoner at once, they secured her tightly and set off for the next town, intending on drawing information from her at any cost. Sorche is unaware that such groups formed because of the chaos and destruction at the hands of Rafe's men, yet none knew where to find him. Thinking she can wheedle her way out of this, she tried to learn all she can and is horrified to discover this particular group is trying to discover Rafe's location so they can exact their vengeance. Sorche knows where Rafe's fortress is located as this is where her sister is also being held. If they get this information from her, she will be of no further use to them, and they can dispatch her at will. She was deathly afraid that her sister will end up paying for her sloppy bungle and can only hope the wizard finds them before the rebels learn of Rafe's location!

Several hours later

"This ought to do it, Lukas. A fine invention, by Neptune's balls!"

And indeed, it was. The light ale was now twice as smooth, with a rich umber colour shining through and a heavy head of foam.

After several rounds of celebratory drinks, Lukas slapped Arcanus on the shoulder.

"Thank ye, man. I pay what I owe. I didn't ken it before, but the witch ye were asking after has been here fo' about three weeks. I had the chambermaid check her room today, but it seems she must ha' slipped out earlier while we were busy tinkering wi' the machine—either that or she's hexed the lot o' us, and for all we know, we could be arse o'er heels under the table and nekkid te boot! The stable lad said he saw her riding out to the next town, Barkeshire, at a leisurely pace, so ye can probably catch up te her."

Arcanus would have been lying if he said he wasn't annoyed to hear that she had been there the entire time, and he'd not known it.

"Thanks, Lukas. I appreciate it. Good luck with your ale!"

He was about to head up to his room and pack when he saw Berik chatting with Lukas. The man nodded to Lukas, then, seeing Arcanus, headed in his direction.

"I hear you're going after the witch," Berik said.

"She's not really a witch, but yes. I have urgent need to find her. What of it?"

Berik shifted, suddenly uncomfortable.

"She has information on the whereabouts of the man who ordered the raid on my village…"

Arcanus was not happy to learn this and became instantly aware that Berik could interfere with his mission. Much as he empathised with the man's loss, he knew what would happen if Berik got to the informer first. He needed to tread carefully.

"Berik, we can travel together in search of her, but I must have your word that you will not harm the woman. She is important to my mission. I would have your word that you will not harm her."

Berik sighed and nodded.

"I have no wish to harm an innocent, Arcanus. Apparently, she is no innocent but an enchantress who ensorcels men…"

Arcanus rubbed his hands over his eyes before fixing them on Berik.

"Your word, Berik."

"Aye, you have my word, friend."

"Since we're about to do this together, let's make plans. I had thought about just traveling after her solo, but it seems like she's a tricky one, so we need to be prepared."

Berik nodded, and the two of them headed to the dining room to make plans. They may as well start tomorrow, seeing that she was looking for him and they were looking for her. Additionally, she didn't know that he and Berik had now teamed up, so if she planned on trapping him, she had another thing coming.

This was going to be an interesting journey, and Arcanus was glad to have an ally to watch his back...

EDICTS OF THE WISE

Delivering Value Through Leadership

Everything we do has value. If we don't understand that value, we can't lead, influence, or drive action. People follow when they see real purpose, not just noise. It's like a business proposal, but bigger than money. Value can be financial, but it can also mean creating safety, stronger communities, better products, smarter governance, efficiency, or long-term stability. Every decision we make as leaders should be tied to delivering real, measurable impact.

Without value, leadership becomes empty. If people don't see the impact of their work, they won't stay motivated. Leaders who can articulate why work matters create stronger teams, drive better outcomes, and build lasting influence. When people know they are working toward something meaningful—whether that's improving a system, solving a problem, or driving innovation—they perform at their best. The work must have purpose, direction, and clarity. Otherwise, it's just noise.

If People Can't See the Value, It Doesn't Exist

Value that isn't visible may as well not exist. If your team doesn't see how their work makes a difference, don't expect them to stay motivated. A leader's job isn't just to create value—it's to make it obvious. Show progress, celebrate wins, and connect the dots between effort and impact. People commit when they can see the difference they're making.

Real Work Needs Real Results

Our work must connect to measurable results. If we can't track the impact, we don't know if we're truly delivering value. It's easy to get caught up in doing things just to look busy, but that doesn't move the needle. Leadership isn't about activity; it's about outcomes. If we're not creating something tangible—better efficiency, stronger teams, higher performance—then what are we actually achieving?

This is why purpose matters. It's not enough to do work for the sake of it. Every project, decision, or action should tie back to a meaningful goal. Leadership is about clarity—making sure every effort contributes to real, measurable change. Whether we create something great or something terrible comes down to our ethics, decisions, and ability to focus on the right things. Real motivation doesn't come from external rewards; it comes from knowing that what we do matters. And when it comes to recognition, don't reward effort—reward the impact through results.

Wisdom Comes From Doing, Not Just Knowing

Wisdom isn't about knowing—it's about doing. You can read books, sit in meetings, and talk theory all day, but until you apply it, you haven't really learned anything. Knowing what to do is easy; actually, doing it is what matters.

You don't get better by waiting for the perfect plan. You get better by taking risks, failing, adjusting, and trying again. If you want to be a strong leader, you need to take action, make decisions, and learn through experience. Leadership isn't about being perfect—it's about learning fast, staying adaptable, and pushing forward despite uncertainty.

Stay Real, Stay Grounded

Don't get lost in the noise or buy into your own hype. Stay real about what you do and why it matters. It's easy to convince yourself you're doing great work when you're just spinning your wheels. Be brutally honest—with yourself and with your team. See things as they are, not just how you want them to be.

The best leaders don't live in an echo chamber. They step outside their own perspective and try to see the world as others do. That's how real insight and smart decisions happen. If people feel like you're getting rewarded differently or chasing your own agenda, they won't trust you. No one follows a leader who's only in it for themselves. To get people behind you, they need to trust that you're leading for the right reasons.

If you want people to back you, they need to know you're making decisions based on what's best for the team or the outcome for your clients, not just yourself. Leadership isn't about looking important—it's about creating value for others. If you're only in it for recognition, power, or status, people will see through it. The best leaders focus on impact, not image.

Leadership Is About Creating the Right Conditions for Others to Succeed

Being able to manage yourself and read the room is one of the most powerful leadership tools you can develop. Leaders who stay calm under pressure, make thoughtful decisions, and build real relationships get the best results. Leadership isn't about having all the answers. It's about creating the right conditions for people to do their best work.

It's not about being the smartest person in the room. It's about making sure everyone in the room can succeed. The most effective leaders remove obstacles, provide clarity, and create momentum. They don't micromanage—they empower. They don't chase credit—they give it. They understand that their success is measured by how well their team performs.

Lead with Purpose, and the Results Will Follow

If you want to be a leader that people respect and follow, focus on value, trust, and impact. Keep learning. Keep improving. Lead with purpose, and the results will follow.

Leadership isn't a title—it's an action. It's not about being in charge; it's about taking responsibility for creating real results. When you focus on value over ego, results over effort, and team success over personal recognition, you become the kind of leader that people want to follow.

The best leaders don't just talk about change—they drive it. They don't just react to challenges—they guide others through them. They don't just set goals—they make sure those goals create meaningful impact.

If you want to lead, start by delivering value. Everything else follows from that.

Value Comes in Many Forms—See Them All

Not all value is obvious, and not all of it is measured in dollars. A strong leader understands that value exists in many forms, and knowing which type to focus on at the right time makes the difference between wasted effort and real impact. The best leaders identify, communicate, and prioritise value to ensure their teams work on what matters most.

A leader who only sees value in revenue or outputs is missing the bigger picture. True leadership understands that value comes in many forms—and knowing when to prioritise which type is what sets great leaders apart.

Not All Value is Good Value—Integrity Comes First

Not all value is worth chasing. If your success comes at the cost of integrity, trust, or people, then it's not value—it's damage. Real leadership isn't just about delivering results; it's about delivering the right results, the right way. If you have to bend ethics to justify an outcome, you're already on the wrong path.

Side Quest
Grain Before Gadgets

The fields stretched endlessly under a golden sun, the tall grass swaying gently in the breeze. As Arcanus and Berik made their way along a dirt path, they spotted a group of villagers clustered around a large wooden structure. From a distance, it looked like a windmill—but as they drew closer, it became clear that something wasn't quite right. The blades were crooked, and the mechanism groaned with each turn.

Berik, always interested in discovering how things worked, stepped forward. "What are you trying to build here?" he asked, his curiosity getting the better of him.

An older woman with calloused hands turned to him, exasperation in her voice. "A mill for grinding grain. We're tired of hauling sacks to the next village, but it's not working properly. The blades don't turn evenly, and the grinding stone keeps jamming."

A younger man, likely the builder, interjected defensively. "It's not that bad! It just needs… a little more time to get it perfect."

Berik tilted his head. "What's your goal here? To build the best mill anyone's ever seen, or to grind grain for the village?"

The young man hesitated. "To grind grain… but if it's not perfect—"

"It doesn't need to be perfect," Berik interrupted, his tone firm. "It needs to work. What's preventing you from making that your number one priority?"

The woman crossed her arms. "He's spent weeks adding fancy mechanisms. Bells, weights, even a whistle to signal when the grain's done grinding. But none of that helps us eat."

Berik nodded. "Right now, you've lost sight of the purpose, Builder. Focus on what adds value—grinding grain. Remove anything that doesn't."

"But what if it fails again?" the builder asked quietly.

"Then you fix it and try again," Berik said. "Failure isn't the enemy here. Not starting, or getting lost in unnecessary details, is."

He turned to the group. "Here's what you'll do: strip it back to the basics. Align the blades, get the grinding stone turning smoothly, and make it functional. Once it works, refine it. Add improvements if they truly help, but your main priority is what serves the village."

The villagers murmured among themselves before nodding. The builder sighed but smiled, seemingly inspired. "Alright. Back to basics."

As they began dismantling the unnecessary mechanisms, Berik stood back, watching them work. "Set a clear objective. Know what success looks like. And if it's not working, adapt."

One of the younger villagers looked up. "You seem to know a lot about building. Where'd you learn it?"

Berik smiled. "Not from mills, but from something similar. I'm a smithy by trade, and that taught me that a flashy suit of armour made from beskar steel is worthless if it doesn't serve its purpose. Sometimes, the simplest solutions are the best.

The young villager frowned. "What's beskar steel?"

"Never mind," Berik said, grinning. "Just remember: results and function first, perfection later."

As he started on his way, a little girl stopped him and handed over a flower as thanks. "Thank you, Mister. You're good at making people get along."

Berik shrugged and patted her head. "It's not hard, little girl. Just ask them what really matters—and then make sure they stick to it."

> "It's not about the money, Patrick.
> It's never been about the money!"
> — National Treasure (Film)

> "We have done the impossible, and that makes us mighty."
> — Firefly (TV Series, Pilot Episode)

Side Quest
The Shipyard Dilemma

Many moons past

The sea breeze carried the faint sound of hammers and saws as the party approached a bustling shipyard along the coast. Ships in various stages of construction dotted the docks, and workers scurried between them like ants. At the centre of the activity stood a half-finished vessel unlike any other: a sleek, innovative design with a curved hull and sails that shimmered like polished steel. Yet, instead of progress, there was tension in the air.

Arcanus paused, observing the scene. "Something isn't right here," he murmured, motioning for his fellow wizard, Bailey, to take the lead.

As they approached, a foreman waved them over, his face lined with frustration. "You're travellers, right? Maybe you can settle a debate. This ship's meant to revolutionise trade routes, but the builders and planners can't agree on how to proceed."

Bailey folded his arms, studying the vessel. "What's the issue?"

The foreman pointed to the workers clustered near the hull. "They're divided. Some want to rush it to sea for testing, others say it's not ready. Meanwhile, the planners keep redesigning the sails, claiming it'll boost speed."

Arcanus nodded, his voice firm. "And what do you think?"

The foreman hesitated. "I think… we're stuck trying to make it perfect, and no one's willing to test what we've already built."

Arcanus stepped closer to the ship, running his hand along the sleek wood. "Perfection doesn't come without trying. You can't know the ship's value until you see how it sails. Stop arguing over what might work and start learning from what does."

The planners muttered among themselves, and one of them spoke up. "But if we test it now and it fails, we waste the effort!"

"Failure isn't a waste—it's how we refine things, how we fix problems," Bailey countered. "Work in smaller steps. Test the hull first, then adjust. Refine the sails in parallel. Progress isn't about doing it all at once; it's about building on what you learn."

Arcanus turned to the foreman, nodding. "You need to connect the team to the purpose. This isn't just a ship—it's a lifeline for faster trade, safer voyages, and stronger ties between ports. Make sure everyone sees that value, not just their own task."

The foreman frowned, his gaze understanding. "You're right. We lost sight of the big picture!"

Arcanus nodded, approving of the conclusion. "Purpose inspires passion, but only when it's clear. Lead with it and avoid the trap of tunnel vision: seeing only what you want to see. Your team needs direction, not delusion."

As the workers began to refocus, Bailey tilted his head toward Arcanus. "You've got a way of snapping them out of it."

Arcanus chuckled. "It's not snapping—it's building. Emotional intelligence is like a ship's keel. You don't see it, but it keeps everything steady."

A young worker ran up, handing Bailey a small wooden model of the ship. "Thank you," he said shyly. "My father and I build these for fun. This one's for you."

Bailey turned the model over in his hands, noting the meticulous detail. "It's beautiful," he said, his smile deepening. "Reminds me of something a master builder would make. Perhaps someone who believes everything is awesome?"

The boy grinned, nodding enthusiastically. As the party left the docks, Bailey placed the model carefully within his robes. "Small pieces, Arcanus," he said softly. "Even the most extraordinary things are built one piece at a time."

A GILDED EDGE

Different ways to consider value

Customer-Driven Value – If it doesn't matter to the customer, does it really matter? The best leaders prioritise customer impact—whether internal or external—because without that, everything else is just self-serving process work.

Risk Reduction Value – Avoiding disaster is just as valuable as creating success. Strong governance, compliance, security, and decision-making prevent problems before they start. Leaders who ignore risk reduction are just rolling the dice.

Productivity & Execution – Getting things done efficiently and effectively is its own kind of value. Leadership isn't about just being busy—it's about making sure the right things are getting done in the smartest way possible.

Business Continuity & Stability – If your organisation or team can't function under pressure, all the success in the world won't matter. Resilience, contingency planning, and adaptability create lasting value when things go wrong.

Safety – Keeping people, systems, and businesses secure isn't a luxury—it's foundational value. A leader who ignores safety isn't leading; they're gambling.

Governance & Compliance – Boring? Maybe. Critical? Absolutely. Governance and compliance create stability, prevent chaos, and protect against long-term risk. Without them, organisations collapse under their own weight.

Efficiency & Simplicity – The easiest way to create value? Remove complexity. A good leader streamlines processes, speeds up decision-making, and removes unnecessary friction so teams can focus on what actually matters.

Human-Centric Change – Value isn't just in the numbers; it's in how people experience change. If you don't bring your people along, even the best ideas will fail. Value isn't just about what gets done—it's about how it gets done.

Eliminating Low-Value Work – Not all work is valuable. Leaders must prioritise high-value activities and cut what doesn't contribute to meaningful outcomes. If a task doesn't create impact, automate it, delegate it, or kill it.

Clarity & Decision-Making – Ambiguity slows everything down. The more clarity a leader provides, the faster people can execute. Clear priorities, expectations, and goals multiply productivity and prevent wasted effort.

Creativity & Innovation – Some value comes from doing things right; other value comes from doing new things. The best leaders balance innovation with execution—pushing for improvement while keeping teams focused on delivering results.

Long-Term Thinking – Some value is immediate, but the best leaders play the long game. Reputation, trust, resilience, and adaptability don't show up in quarterly reports, but they determine who thrives and who burns out.

Resilience & Continuity – Can your team, system, or organisation handle a crisis? If not, no other value matters. Stability and the ability to weather storms is one of the most underrated leadership values.

Knowledge & Learning – Every decision either adds to or depletes collective intelligence. Leaders who invest in learning, upskilling, and capturing knowledge create lasting value. Those who ignore it leave their teams scrambling in the dark.

Relationships & Trust – You can't lead without trust. Strong relationships within and outside your team build reputation, influence, and credibility—all of which are invaluable assets that money can't buy.

Speed & Agility – Value isn't just about what gets done, but how quickly you can adapt. In a fast-moving world, the ability to pivot, seize opportunities, and make decisions before they're forced upon you is a competitive advantage.

Employee Well-Being – A burnt-out, disengaged team delivers zero value. Protecting energy, focus, and mental resilience ensures your team can deliver sustainable, long-term results.

Sustainability & Responsibility – If you're only thinking about today's success, you're ignoring tomorrow's survival. Whether it's operational efficiency, financial sustainability, or responsible decision-making, real leaders build for the future, not just the now.

THE UNWRITTEN RULES

People Won't Follow You Unless They See That You're Driving Value for Them, Not Just Yourself

People don't commit to leaders who are only in it for themselves. They follow when they see that your leadership benefits them—their growth, their work, their success. If you're making decisions based only on what looks good for you, expect loyalty to disappear fast.

Logic Alone Doesn't Motivate People—Emotional Buy-In is Key

People don't get behind facts—they get behind stories, meaning, and purpose. If you want commitment, don't just present the numbers—people feel why it matters. If they don't care about the outcome, they won't push for it.

Value Without Execution is Just a Nice Idea

You can have the best strategy, the clearest vision, and the most compelling mission, but if you can't turn those into actual outcomes, they mean nothing. People follow results, not empty talk. A leader's job isn't just to talk about value—it's to make sure aligned results happen.

People Care About How You Make Them Feel, Not Just What You Deliver

You can be the smartest person in the room, but if people feel unheard, dismissed, or undervalued, they won't work with you for long. Your value isn't just in the results—it's in how you treat people along the way. Respect, recognition, and genuine human connection go further than any achievement.

THE MIRROR OF MASTERY

» How do I shift from being a high-performing individual contributor to a leader whose success is measured by the results of the team?

» How do I ensure that my leadership creates an environment where the team and I are focused on high-value work?

» How do I build trust, fairness, and strong relationships so that my team is motivated to follow me?

CHAPTER 3

The Road Ahead – Trusting Instincts and Allies

Main Quest

The Odyssey of Purposeful Leadership

After leaving the village of Elipa behind, Arcanus and his companions started making tracks for the next town on their maps: Bassel. They were sure she was headed toward Novia, a beautiful and scenic lagoon city that rivalled the beauty of Loria. It was said that Novia had been built as a tribute by its first King, Jakob, for his wife, Queen Michaela, upon the birth of his son and heir, Horus. A marvellous feat of ingenuity, if true…

They had been following tracks for several days, and on the third, it looked like they had come across their first clue—confirmation that they were on the right track. The innkeeper had provided a description of the woman, including what she was wearing. He noted that she had worn an unusual bracelet made of a silvery, almost filmy material that turned all the colours of the rainbow in the light.

Just their luck! It was her bracelet. Berik's keen eyes had spotted something shimmering in the shrubs, and upon closer inspection, it seemed their thief might now be a hostage herself. A scattered old campfire and the remains of a camp housing maybe fifteen to twenty members only added to Arcanus's growing excitement. Berik must have noticed, because he started frowning.

"I don't like this, Arcanus. This feels like a trap, like someone deliberately left this for us to find…"

Arcanus stopped short as Berik's words sank in. He was

right. There was something off about this whole situation, but they couldn't ignore the clue—the entire world was at risk. He knew he didn't have to remind Berik of that, as the man was already well aware of who the enemy was and what power he held.

Berik was also a seasoned warrior, with great instincts, and if they were screaming out at him, Arcanus trusted them too. He recalled the High Elder speaking to them about leadership—how to curate good relationships within a team while maintaining clear boundaries and accountability.

Flashback – sixteen-year-old Arcanus

"So, students, which path do you choose?" The instructor's voice carried across the hall like the toll of an ancient bell, steady and measured. "You have been summoned to solve a problem. You have gathered your allies, and each knows their place in the grand design. As their leader, it falls upon you to understand their strengths and guide them well. You are their steward, their shield when needed, and the voice that calls them to action. You must stand apart—approachable, yet unwavering.

"There will be moments of triumph when your words inspire, and there will be moments of hardship when steel is required instead of song. A leader does not falter in either.

"As you tread this path, you will notice that those who follow you often fall into two broad camps. Some take a proactive stance, ever seeking mastery, pushing beyond mere expectation, honing their craft with foresight and discipline. They do not wait for obstacles to rise—they anticipate them and prepare accordingly.

"Others take a transactional approach. They fulfil their tasks as assigned, precise and steady, meeting expectations without seeking beyond them. This is neither folly nor failure—such roles have their place, and without them, kingdoms would crumble. But those who would captain a journey must understand the difference, for it will shape the battles they fight and the victories they claim."

A hush settled over the chamber as the instructor let his words breathe. Then, with deliberate patience, his gaze found Arcanus.

"Arcanus, once you have finished your great excavation there, perhaps you might enlighten the class. What, pray tell, do you believe I meant by that statement? Assuming, of course, that you were paying attention..."

Arcanus turned a shade of crimson. He yanked his offending finger away as if it had been caught in a fae trap. It wasn't his fault, someone had hexed him with a booger-me-all-the-time curse, and he was fairly certain the situation was escalating. What if the accursed things grew so large they split his nose in two?!

"Apologies, sir! No offense intended, just dealing with an... ongoing affliction."

The instructor arched a brow. "You are welcome to wage that battle—in your own time."

Arcanus swallowed hard, straightened his robes, and did his best to salvage his dignity. "Sir, a proactive approach would be akin to my work as a wizard specialising in grand celebrations. I craft events for kings, noble houses, and merchants alike. But orchestrating a festival is more than just executing the plan at hand. It requires foresight, preparation, and adaptability.

"If I intend to showcase animated ice sculptures at a grand banquet, I must think ahead: What if the cooling enchantment falters? Do I have a backup plan? What if the spell woven into the sky-lanterns wanes before the feast reaches its crescendo? A proactive leader does not wait for disaster to strike—they prepare for its arrival before it ever darkens the door.

"Now, compare that to a transactional approach, such as a clerk in a wand repair shop. A customer presents a broken wand, the clerk issues a claim ticket, and their work is done. They address only the task before them, never looking beyond its immediate scope. This is not wrong, nor is it without purpose. Such roles exist in every city, every guild, every army, every village. But where one must lead, where one must rise beyond the simple act of duty, this mindset can become constraining.

"A leader must understand both approaches. A wand clerk, for instance, may remain strictly transactional, or they may take a step beyond. Stepping up, advising a customer on how to prevent future breakages, ensuring their craft serves not just for the moment, but for what comes next. In that moment, they transcend their station—they evolve."

The instructor gave a slow nod. "A well-reasoned answer, Arcanus. It is good to see that beneath your distractions, your mind is still sharp."

He turned his gaze back to the assembled students. "Now, Arcanus has illuminated a key truth—awareness. It is not enough to act; one must perceive.

"Some of you believe that knowledge will seep into you as if by osmosis, that presence alone is enough. But I tell you this: true learning is forged, not found. If you fail to listen, you will assume. And assumptions, dear students, are the fastest road to ruin.

"How often have you misunderstood an order because your mind wandered elsewhere? How many times have you hesitated to ask for clarity, only to find yourself lost in the very task you sought to avoid questioning?

"As leaders, as wayfarers on paths yet unseen, it is not enough to understand only yourself, you must understand those around you. You must recognise when a companion is faltering, when their grasp on the lesson is slipping. It is your duty to ask: Are they following? Have I made myself clear? If confusion lingers, what can I do to illuminate the path?

"And make no mistake, this is no mere classroom exercise.

"There will come a day when you stand in the halls of a foreign court, where a single word misspoken could turn allies to enemies. You may be sent as envoys to uneasy factions, where your ability to read the air between them determines whether peace prevails or war ignites.

"Your capacity to listen, to perceive, to adapt, will shape your fate.

"So, reflect well. How do you carry yourself? What can you refine? What steps must you take to master clarity, both in thought and in action?

"This is not a mere exercise in leadership. In the wrong moment, it may be the difference between victory and exile—between honour and the headsman's blade."

"The key is in not spending time, but in investing it."

"Begin with the end in mind."

"Your most important work is always ahead of you, never behind you."

"Leadership is communicating to people their worth and potential so clearly that they come to see it in themselves."

"Accountability breeds response ability."

> *"Trust is the glue of life. It is the most essential ingredient in effective communication. It is the foundational principle that holds all relationships together."*
>
> *"Live out of your imagination, not your history."*
>
> — Stephen R. Covey, The 7 Habits of Highly Effective People

Thinking back on what his teacher had taught him, Arcanus decided to ask Berik's opinion on the best way forward, especially since this was his forte. While Arcanus remained the mission leader, Berik's experience was invaluable.

"What do you think, Berik? How should we proceed?"

Berik was silent and thoughtful. His silence made Arcanus jumpy, and his feet started pacing on the spot—a bad habit. Berik noticed and frowned, his travel-weary, dust-coated face and reddened eyes filled with annoyance. Arcanus stopped and chuckled. "Sorry…"

"When we get to the next town, we should be careful who we make our inquiries to. If we're not discreet, we could be falling into a trap that ends with both of us—and your magyck stick—being carted off to that bastard, Rafe. I think we should split up on the town's border, keep a low profile, and see what we see."

Arcanus nodded, but Berik snorted.

"I mean it, Arcanus. Don't go around making improvements like you do—that will only draw attention to yourself."

"It's my nature to help, Berik, but I hear you. I promise to sit tight. Perhaps, you can do a good turn instead?"

Berik snorted again, mumbling under his breath, "Ain't got the time for that right now…"

They got back on their horses and continued the journey, hoping to come across the group before they reached the town, where the danger level to the local population was tenfold more.

Alas, their luck had run out, and they travelled several more days, finally reaching the town of Dwerry—a halfway point between them and the Lagoon City.

Arcanus procured rooms for them and decided to take an early night. He trusted Berik when he said he would handle the first night's investigation, and as Arcanus lay back on the cool sheets of his comfortable bed, with the full moon's light gliding in through the cool night air, he thought about how proud the High Elder would be.

He was actively listening to his team, and they to him. He trusted them to do their job, and though he was familiar with all aspects and details this trip could potentially take, he was pleased to see Berik taking a proactive approach.

For the first time in many days, Arcanus fell into a deep and untroubled sleep.

> "Your job as a leader is not to do the work, it is to create an environment where the work gets done."
>
> "If you are constantly stepping in to fix problems, your people will let you. And you will end up doing their jobs, not yours."
>
> "If you are running over the top of your peers, you are not leading, you are just being a control freak."
>
> "You need to operate at your altitude. Do not punch above your weight unless you have been invited to do so."
>
> "Leadership is not about being liked; it is about making the best decisions."
>
> "If you keep stepping in to rescue your team, you are stopping them from learning and growing."

> *"It is not about you. The best leaders make it about the mission, the team, and the outcomes."*
>
> — Martin G. Moore, No Bullsh!t Leadership

Meanwhile, across town in a dirty storehouse, Sorche sat tightly bound and watched over by the remaining rebels. Traveling for days like a trussed-up chicken had been hard, but she had made certain not to complain too much—she had to find a way out of here if that useless wizard hadn't managed to find her clue.

"Why'd I leave my bracelet," she moaned sadly.

At least these ruffians left her alone for the most part…

Berik had pulled his cowl over his face as he sat in a dark corner of the inn's public room, listening to the gossip. So far, he'd heard more than he wanted to from a busty barmaid looking to tup him in her room on the servant's floor. He grunted his disgust, but that clearly excited her further as she kept bringing him cup after cup of free ale.

"Silly wench," he mumbled, taking another sip from his mug of water. He needed a clear head for this. It suddenly occurred to him that perhaps someone aside from the barmaid wanted him inebriated—perhaps someone had been watching for their arrival at the town's gates…

He pushed himself further back into the corner and waited. He knew from previous visits that this was the place to be after dark, as all the men gathered here to drink and wench their way through the night. It was just a matter of time before the group of bandits revealed themselves. All he had to do was read the room and wait for answers to be served up.

He was not disappointed. Several minutes later, a group of dirty, dishevelled men stumbled in, loud and drunk. Two of them started arguing over who would have the first go with the barmaid, who looked none too pleased about either prospect.

"I tell un I wan' go first. I been lookin' afer that there skinny wench for days, and boss said I canna tup her. I was the only one lef' behin' when yer went to town afore this. 'Tis my turn te be first now, Norris!"

The man called Norris, an ugly blighter if there ever was one, grunted and ploughed his head into his companion's belly, knocking him into the wall. The rest of their friends laughed and shrugged, turning back to their amusements and drink. Norris, the clear winner, grabbed hold of the barmaid's hand and took off upstairs.

Berik's eyes narrowed as he focused on the companion, who was now painfully pulling himself upright. This was his chance. He raised his glass of water to the man and waved him over, pointing to the untouched glasses of ale on his table. The companion gave him a rough, toothless smile and made his way over, glad for what he saw as a small victory—free ale!

"Welcome, friend. Have a seat and grab a mug," Berik said casually.

"Thanks, mate. Name's Jimi. Wats yers?"

"Call me Bob. I'm sorry your friend took your girl away from you..."

Jimi finished his first mug of ale and grabbed a second, spitting as he did so.

"He's no fren' o' mine. We's just workin' together for a job. I hate the blighter, I do."

"I'm sure... What brings you around these parts?"

"We's transportin' goods for the gov. Norris here is the gov's man, and most o' the men are his, so's I can' exactly lop his nob off an' be done wi' it. Took us weeks te get the cargo in the first place. Mind you, the wench he took upsta—"

Berik tuned out. He had learned what he needed—these were the enchantress's kidnappers for sure. But now what? They were outnumbered—two against twenty—and if his drunk companion was right, they were trained warriors. The chances of winning had decreased some.

Alright, more than "some," but Berik couldn't give up the chance to exact his revenge on the men responsible for killing his family, burning his village, and the man who had ordered the lot of it done. He had the information, and it was important—but what was the next step?

Berik sat and watched as his companion inhaled mug after mug of ale, deciding it was now or never. He had considered waking Arcanus and relaying the information, but he didn't want to waste a second. And if he were being truthful, while Arcanus was a good fighter, he would probably just get in the way.

"Say, friend. Would you like me to help you home?"

"N-no thanks, goo' man. The rest of my group's here, so I hafta wait for 'em. Besides, I been starin' at those storehouse walls for a few days, though I was gon' go mad every time that stupid horn blew!"

It was then that Berik understood the location of said storehouse—near the town's gates, by the east entrance.

Berik decided to be proactive and take extra measures to secure their target and her safety. He motioned for the innkeeper, Acton—a man he knew and respected. He would leave a note for Arcanus, and Acton would see it delivered himself. The note would explain everything he had learned and the plan he had formulated, plus the location of the storehouse.

Seeing that he had extracted all the information he

could from Jimi, and knowing that the bandits would all be dead drunk by the end of the evening, Berik set off for the storehouse.

He had anticipated his moves and any possible challenges that might arise, including an unexpected ambush by an outside spotter watching the storehouse, and had relayed instructions to Arcanus. Each man had a job to do, and if Berik wanted this plan to succeed, he had to make sure each step was carefully followed.

He knew Arcanus was the mission's leader overall, but he also understood that when it came to challenges and sticky situations such as this, he would take point. He knew Arcanus would appreciate his input, support, and plan, as it positioned them well—taking into account the bigger picture: the mission's safety and the recovery of the skrol.

About twenty-five minutes later, Berik saw the shape of the storehouse against the night sky and smiled grimly. It was time to scout the area and remove any potential spotters—before they could warn the men inside.

Yes, things were going according to plan.

EDICTS OF THE WISE

Stay in Your Lane—Lead with Clarity and Purpose

We are hired to do a job, not someone else's. That's why roles, responsibilities, and structure exist—so the whole system works. If everyone delivers results in their own area, things run smoothly. The best leaders focus on what they were brought in to do—and do it well.

Your main responsibility is to be rock solid at your level. If you constantly step into your team's work, take over your peers' responsibilities, or try to do your boss's job without being invited, you're not leading—you're distracting yourself from where you need to be. Great leadership is about operating at the right altitude.

Leadership isn't just about staying in your lane—it's about knowing when to step beyond it. But don't expect a warm welcome every time you do. Moving into someone else's space—whether above, below, or beside you—will always bring some resistance. People are protective of their roles. At the same time, those above you will take notice when you proactively solve problems, show initiative, and add value in ways that respect the structure. That's how you earn the right to take on more responsibility.

Micromanagement Isn't Leadership—It's Interference

If you're constantly stepping into your team's work, you're not leading—you're limiting. Micromanagement signals a lack of trust, kills autonomy, and slows progress. Your job isn't to do their job. It's to set expectations, provide guidance, and then let them deliver. If you don't trust them to do their work, ask yourself why you hired them.

Learn the System—But Don't Force Your Way In

Learning never stops. If you want to grow, you need to understand how your role connects to others. But there's a difference between being curious and being intrusive. You can observe, ask questions, and offer help when the opportunity is there. But you can't force your way in. You have to be invited, and your input has to be wanted.

This means you need clarity and active listening. If you don't understand what's happening around you, you'll make bad assumptions. If you don't listen, you'll miss key signals about when to step up, when to step back, and when to stay put. Leadership is about reading the room and knowing when to act.

Boundaries Are the Foundation of Leadership

Managing boundaries—both personal and professional—is non-negotiable. It's easy to overstep when you're eager to contribute, but leadership is about knowing when to push forward and when to hold back. A great leader doesn't take over someone else's job. They create clarity, empower others, and ensure the right people are delivering results in their own lanes.

At the same time, we need to be clear on why and when to shift lanes. Whether it's a promotion, a new opportunity, or a strategic move, we can't jump around just for the sake of it. Changing lanes has to be intentional, backed by results, and aligned with our ability to deliver at that next level.

Look Beyond the Immediate—Be Proactive, Not Just Transactional

There's a difference between being transactional and being proactive. If you only focus on what's in front of you, you'll always be stuck reacting. Leadership is about seeing the bigger picture, anticipating future challenges, and making strategic moves before they're needed.

The best leaders think ahead. They connect the dots. They position themselves for what comes next.

Before stepping into a new space, understand your motivation. Authenticity is everything. If you're pushing into a new area for the wrong reasons—whether it's ego, control, or recognition—it will backfire. But if you're expanding your influence with a genuine intent to contribute, support, and elevate others, that's when real leadership happens.

The Higher You Go, the More You Deliver the Results Through Others

Leadership shifts as you move up. The higher you go, the less you achieve through your own hands and the more you achieve through your team. Leadership isn't about doing more work—it's about enabling others to succeed.

But leadership isn't just about the top—it happens at every level. The best leaders master their current level before moving up. If you can't drive results where you are, you won't be effective at the next stage. Leadership is earned through execution, not entitlement.

Setting the tone and expectations for your lane means aligning everything with the results needed to achieve the bigger mission. It's not about setting rules just to have rules—it's about creating clarity. When everyone understands the standards, expectations, and outcomes that matter most, they can focus on delivering results.

Technical Knowledge vs. Leadership: Understanding Without Doing

Knowing the technical without doing the technical is a crucial leadership skill. Take Elon Musk as an example—he's deeply technical, but he doesn't build rockets himself. Future leaders, especially in technical fields, need to be engineers first, leaders second. They need to understand the fundamentals so they can challenge assumptions, drive innovation, and make informed decisions.

But leadership isn't about being the smartest person in the room—it's about enabling the smartest people in the room to do their best work. The best leaders ask the right questions, provide the right support, and clear the path for their teams.

Trust Matters More Than Friendship

Friendly but not friends. Professional boundaries matter. Great leaders build strong, trust-based relationships, but they don't blur the lines. When leaders become too personally involved, it can create bias, favouritisms, or an inability to make tough calls.

Leadership requires respect, fairness, and clear separation between personal and professional dynamics. If people trust you, they will follow you—even if you're not their friend.

Big-Picture Leadership: Aligning Value Across All Lanes

Setting vision and purpose means aligning results with value and shaping how things are done across all levels. Leadership at this level isn't just about managing your own lane—it's about influencing the broader system and ensuring others are set up for success.

A strong vision doesn't just provide direction—it creates clarity for others, helping them understand how their work fits into the bigger picture. The best leaders don't just execute—they shape the environment so that others can perform at their best.

Great Leaders Shape Change, Not Just React to It

Life is uncertain, and change is constant. The best leaders don't resist it—they lean into it. The world isn't fixed, and neither are the challenges we face. Instead of reacting to change, great leaders define it.

They see opportunities where others see obstacles. They don't just navigate uncertainty—they turn ambiguity into progress. Leadership is about being decisive in chaos and strategic in uncertainty.

Leadership Is Influence—And Influence Is Sales

Sales isn't just for sales teams. As a leader, you're always selling—selling the vision internally so your team believes in it, commits to it, and takes ownership of it. If your team doesn't buy in, they won't give their best.

You're also selling externally—whether to stakeholders, executives, or clients. No matter how great your strategy is, if you can't communicate it in a way that inspires action, it won't get traction.

Leadership is about influence, and influence is about selling the right idea to the right people at the right time.

Sales is not sleazy or manipulative; it's demonstrating that we have something valuable that other people need.

Management and leadership are not the same.

A manager makes sure that the ladder is sturdy, the rungs are in good shape, and everyone is climbing efficiently. A leader steps back and asks, 'Is the ladder even against the right wall?' Management is about optimising processes, maintaining order, and ensuring execution. Leadership is about setting the right direction, making sure effort aligns with purpose, and questioning whether what we're doing is even the right thing. A great leader doesn't just keep people moving—they make sure they're moving toward something that matters.

Lead with Clarity, Purpose, and Ownership

The best leaders don't just manage a function, a technology, a team, or work—they create clarity, drive results, and inspire action. They don't just react to change—they shape it. They are about delivering results that drive value at every level. Do that well, and everything else falls into place.

Side Quest
The Harvest Will Not Wait

The sun hung low over the plains as Arcanus and Berik crested a hill, looking down on a small settlement surrounded by fields of golden grain. Smoke curled lazily from a blacksmith's forge, and the sounds of shouting carried up to them. Berik squinted at the commotion below.

"Sounds like they've hit a snag," he muttered to Arcanus.

As they approached, they found a group of villagers gathered around a strange contraption—a crude threshing machine, half-built in the middle of the field. Tools lay scattered, and tempers flared as two men argued while others stood by, unsure whether to intervene.

"What's going on here?" Arcanus asked, stepping forward.

The older of the two men, a wiry figure with a streak of grease on his cheek, gestured at the contraption. "This machine was supposed to speed up the harvest, but it's not working. We can't agree on how to fix it."

The younger man, arms crossed, scoffed. "Fix it? It wasn't even built right to start with!"

Arcanus raised a hand, silencing them. "Enough. Let's get to the root of this. What's the machine supposed to do?"

"Separate the grain from the stalks," the older man replied. "If we can't get it working, we'll lose time, and the rains might ruin the harvest."

Berik walked around the machine, examining its components with a practiced eye. "Alright, it's clear this needs some work before it's operational again. Before we dig into the how, let's set a few ground rules." He turned to Arcanus, who nodded in encouragement. Planting himself firmly, Berik addressed the gathered villagers.

"You're all here for the same goal: the harvest. No more pointing fingers. Stay in your lane—do the part you're best at and trust the others to do theirs."

The older man bristled. "But if they mess up—"

"Then it's on me," Berik interrupted. "I'll guide you, but I won't be turning every bolt myself. I know enough to spot mistakes, but not enough to do your jobs better than you can. That's why you're here."

The group quieted as Berik continued. "We don't need perfection. Focus on the essentials—what gets this machine running well enough to save the harvest. Leave the extras for later. Do that, and we'll all come out ahead."

The younger man hesitated, then asked, "What if it still doesn't work?"

"Then we adapt and adjust," Berik said. "The alternative is to stand here arguing and lose everything. Let's move."

Under Berik's guidance, the villagers divided tasks: the smith repaired the bent metal supports, the carpenter adjusted the wooden frame, and the young man fine-tuned the mechanism. By nightfall, the machine groaned to life, threshing grain with an uneven but functional rhythm.

As they tested the first batch, the older man approached Berik. "You managed to pull this lot together. How'd you do it?"

Berik smirked. "Same way Nehemiah rebuilt the walls—set clear expectations, stayed in my lane, and trusted the team to do the rest."

The man frowned. "Nehemiah?"

Berik chuckled. "Never mind. Just know this: good leaders build, but they don't lay every stone. Remember that."

As they moved on, Arcanus glanced at Berik. "Biblical references? You're full of surprises."

Berik shrugged, his hammer swinging at his side. "Lessons that last are worth repeating, no matter where they come from. Now, let's get moving before the rains catch us."

> *"You can't go this far and not go further."*
> — Hank Scorpio, The Simpsons
> (Season 8, Episode 2, You Only Move Twice)

Side Quest
Seeing Beyond the Storm

A few hours ago

The roar of waves echoed off the cliffs as the party arrived at Dwerry. Fishing nets hung in tangled piles, and a group of villagers stood near an incomplete lighthouse, arguing furiously. Arcanus stepped forward, his eyes narrowing as he surveyed the scene.

A wiry young man, clearly the architect, was gesturing at the lighthouse. "If we don't finish the tower with reinforced stone, it'll collapse during the next storm!"

An older sailor, his face weathered by the sea, jabbed a finger at the architect. "And how do we pay for it? The traders won't invest in a lighthouse they don't think we need. We're better off patching the old beacon!"

Arcanus raised a hand, silencing them. "Good day, gentlemen. It seems you're losing focus. Why is this lighthouse here? What's its purpose?"

"To guide ships safely to harbour," the architect replied immediately. "And to attract larger vessels that bring trade."

Arcanus nodded. "Exactly. It's more than just a lighthouse—it's the foundation of this village's future. Without it, no one prospers."

The sailor crossed his arms. "That's fine talk, but if it's not done in time, the next storm will ruin what little we've built."

"Then we need a plan," Arcanus said. "Here's the plan: build the lighthouse in stages. Finish the foundation with what you have—enough to stand through storms. Use that to show the traders the potential—sell them the future. They'll invest when they see it can weather the tides."

The architect hesitated. "What if they don't invest?"

Arcanus turned to him with an understanding smile. "Then we adapt. Life is uncertain, but you don't stop shaping the world because of doubt. Show them the value. Convince them that this lighthouse isn't just for today, but for generations."

The group exchanged glances, then nodded. As they began dividing tasks, the sailor muttered, "And what if storms sink us before we finish?"

Berik rolled his eyes. "Then you've built the foundations to start again. But doing nothing guarantees failure." He paused, his voice lowering. "You've seen the game—now play it smarter."

The architect glanced at him, puzzled. "Game?"

"Sometimes the only winning move is to play differently," Berik said, quoting an old strategist's teaching. "Now get to it."

As the party left to hunt out an inn or boarding house, Arcanus raised an eyebrow. "That line about playing smarter—where did you learn that?"

"From a copper contraption that learned how to think,"

Berik said, his tone light. "Sometimes you don't win by playing the expected game. You win by shaping the rules."

The cliffs faded into the horizon as they moved on, leaving the villagers to their work and the lighthouse to an uncertain future. Within a few minutes, Arcanus had secured them rooms and decided to take an early night. He trusted Berik when he said to leave the first night's investigation to him, and as Arcanus lay back on the cool sheets of his comfortable bed, with the full moon's light gliding in through the cool night air, he thought about how proud the High Mage would be.

He was actively listening to his team, trusting them to do their job, and not taking on or shouldering all the responsibility himself, though he knew it was within his skillset.

For the first time in many days, Arcanus fell into a deep and untroubled sleep.

A GILDED EDGE

Understanding Roles in an Organisation: Rock Stars, Managers, and Leaders

In any organisation, the way we operate within our roles tends to fall into three primary categories: Rock Stars, Managers, and Leaders. These roles overlap in different ways, and individuals can embody different percentages of each depending on their strengths, responsibilities, and career path. Understanding these distinctions helps us navigate where we add the most value and how we grow.

Rock Stars: Masters of Their Craft

Rock Stars are the foundation of any successful team. They are high-performing individuals who excel in their role, stay focused on their lane, and deliver consistently strong results. They don't necessarily manage others or drive strategy, but they are trusted, reliable, and exceptional at what they do. Some Rock Stars stay in this lane their entire careers—and that's a good thing. Every organisation needs people who just get the job done, at a high level, without distraction.

Managers: Keeping the System Running and is cared for

Managers bridge the gap between execution and structure. Their role is to ensure their area runs efficiently, stays on track, and functions smoothly. Management can take many forms—you can be a manager of people, processes, technology, or operations. The key focus is on maintenance and optimisation. Managers ensure that things don't break down, teams stay aligned, and output remains stable. However, management alone is not leadership—it's about stability, not necessarily innovation or direction.

Leaders: Direction and Influence

Leaders operate on a different dimension. While managers ensure things run well, leaders determine where things should go. Leadership is about influence, vision, and change. A leader guides direction, rallies people toward a cause, and drives evolution rather than just maintaining the status quo. Some leaders also manage, but leadership is not dependent on a title—it's about how much impact someone has on shaping the future.

Beyond Employees: Freelancers and Entrepreneurs

While most people fit into Rock Star, Manager, or Leader roles inside organisations, some operate outside traditional employment structures.

Freelancers exchange time for money, much like employees, but typically with a transactional focus. Their job is to deliver a service, not to manage or lead within a company's structure.

Entrepreneurs are visionaries, often weighted more toward leadership than management. They are idea-driven, influence-heavy, and focused on creating new things rather than maintaining existing structures. Entrepreneurs thrive on risk, growth, and bringing others along for the ride, heavy emphasis on time buy back and bringing people in to execute.

Understanding the Mix: Finding Your Balance

Most roles aren't purely one thing. You can be a Rock Star Manager, meaning you excel at both execution and keeping things running. You can be a manager with leadership tendencies, guiding teams while also structuring them efficiently. The key is understanding where your time is spent and how your skill set fits into the bigger picture.

For example, you might be an incredible technical or trade manager running a system efficiently but not heavily focused on leadership. Or you could be a highly skilled Rock Star employee who doesn't manage or lead—but your expertise makes you indispensable. Paradox: be a rock star manager or leader all wrapped up in one.

Own Your Role and Play It Well

Every successful organisation needs a balance of Rock Stars, Managers, and Leaders. There's no single best role—only the best role for you with in your professional roles and responsibilities. The key to growth is knowing where you stand, where you want to be, and how to leverage your strengths to drive impact. Whether you're a Rock Star at execution, a Manager ensuring smooth operation, or a Leader shaping direction, the best results come from owning your space and delivering at the highest level.

THE UNWRITTEN RULES

Not Everyone Thinks Like You—Start Simple

Just because something makes sense to you doesn't mean it does to others. Some people need broad ideas first before they can engage with details. If you start with the fine print, you'll lose them before they care. Big picture first, next steps second, details last.

What People Say Isn't Always What They Mean

Words are just one part of communication. Tone, body language, and intent matter just as much. When someone says, "It's fine," they might mean anything from "This is great" to "I hate it, but I don't want to argue." Listen beyond the words.

Repetition Builds Alignment—Once Isn't Enough

Saying something once isn't communication—it's an announcement. If you want people to align with your vision, say it again, then say it differently—meetings, emails, casual conversations. Clarity comes from reinforcement, not assumption.

Trust Wins Followers, Not Just Intelligence

Being the smartest in the room doesn't mean people will follow you. They follow leaders they trust. If you ignore relationships and rely on logic alone, you'll be respected but not influential. People commit to leaders who listen, keep their word, and take an interest, proving they care.

THE MIRROR OF MASTERY

» When I communicate an idea or vision, do I focus more on logic and details, or do I consider how others might connect with it emotionally or in a relatable way?

» How do I distinguish when I should take control of a situation versus when I should step back and allow others to take ownership?

» In what ways do I unintentionally create barriers between myself and others, and how can I adjust while still being authentic?

CHAPTER 4

Gold, Greed, and the Bonds of Truth

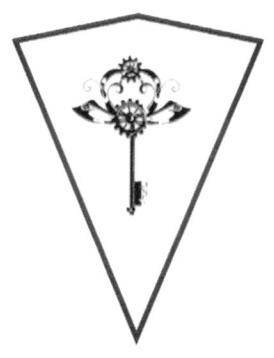

Main Quest

The Odyssey of Purposeful Leadership

Arcanus stirred in bed and sat up, smiling. He turned toward the open window and noticed the sky was turning a delicate pink tinged with orange, yellow, and pale shades of blue. The air was crisp and clear, almost sweet. What a wonderful, peaceful sleep. He hoped Berik had a good night; otherwise, he'd feel guilty over this—even if he did volunteer...

After spending several more minutes at the window, Arcanus turned—and froze. A note had been slipped under the door sometime during the night. He sprinted over and, after taking a deep breath, started to read. It was in Berik's hand, and it seemed that while Arcanus had been holidaying in Lala land, Berik had managed to locate the girl and determine where she was being held.

Additionally, Berik mentioned that at least half the group had passed out cold from the previous night's revelries. He had set out for the storehouse the night before to scout for any spotters who might ambush them and would be waiting for the cavalry—aka Arcanus—to show up after his "beauty sleep."

The man was chiding him.

For a moment, Arcanus felt irked that Berik had made several decisions without consulting him. But he knew that was his pride talking. As a leader who trusted his team, he was glad Berik felt safe enough to make decisions, reason out a plan, fine-tune it, and move forward. It meant that Arcanus was growing as well—trusting himself more in selecting the right people not only to handle tasks but to plan them and see them through.

He had been clear with his instructions, and Berik had followed through. *Good on both of us.*

He wondered how the rest of the day would go…

Arcanus hurried to wash and dress, thankful that a warm bowl of fresh water had been placed outside his door. Had someone opened that door to leave the water inside, that note might have been dislodged and lost!

After throwing yesterday's clothes into his backpack, he made tracks downstairs, taking care to thank the innkeeper for his discretion—and for the breakfast pie he munched on the way out to the stable. His horse had finished its breakfast and was enjoying a leisurely groom.

"You lucky devil," Arcanus chuckled as he quickly saddled the horse.

They were on the road in a few minutes. Referring back to Berik's note, he noted that Berik had suggested taking a back road to the storehouse—the main road was too exposed, and they would see someone coming a mile away.

The man had thought of everything, Arcanus marvelled. Though in reality, they had both set ground rules about keeping a low profile.

Nevertheless, he resolved to stay extra vigilant on the back road.

Berik watched the narrow back road from his position high up in a tree, overlooking the path in one direction with a clear view of the storehouse in the other. He would see

Arcanus coming with plenty of time to spare, and thankfully, he had already dispatched the two spotters waiting around the storehouse.

Bad luck, though. They had been hired mercs, not part of the main team.

"Which means we'll be fighting around seven to ten men, give or take…" Berik muttered to himself before groaning and rubbing his sore behind. Nesting in the tree for the past couple of hours had been hellish, and he was sure he would pay for it later.

A soft nicker caught his attention. Watching the road, he saw Arcanus carefully guiding his horse across the stony ground, ensuring he made no loud movements or drew any unwanted attention.

"Good man," Berik nodded to himself.

He silently leapt down from the tree and caught Arcanus's eye. Without a word, he led him to a small overgrowth of bushes, and stepping around it, Arcanus saw Berik's horse. The area was wide enough to safely shelter two horses—away from prying eyes and thieving hands—while they focused on the task ahead.

"Thanks for the note and the details. I must say, I'm impressed you've planned everything so carefully…" Arcanus remarked.

Berik rolled his eyes. "You know I'm a skilled strategist, Arcanus…"

"Yeah, I do, but I'm just voicing my respect and support for this plan. One thing though, Berik—now that we're on the verge of capturing her, I must ask that you remember your vow to me. Do not lose your cool. I'm being as clear and direct as possible so there is no possibility of miscommunication. We cannot let anyone from Rafe's gang know who we are or why we want the girl. If I'm right—and I'm pretty sure I am—the girl left that clue for us to find her. She knew we were her only way out."

Berik surprised Arcanus by simply nodding, and he marvelled at yet another Academy lesson playing out perfectly. By being upfront, owning his words with integrity, and not manipulating or twisting them to get the outcome he desired, Arcanus opened himself up to his partner.

This allowed Berik to see him for him—to understand that while Arcanus respected his input, he would put his foot down where necessary, especially when it came to the safety of this mission.

Radical candor was an odd duck. It could be an uncomfortable space for many leaders who struggled with managing the fine line between brutal honesty and cruelty.

"Now that that's sorted, how do you want to proceed?" Arcanus asked.

"I believe a distraction is needed since we don't know how well they're armed," Berik replied. "I've seen a few step outside to take a piss in the woods, and they only had a sword on them, but I am 100% sure they have more than swords at hand. We need to be careful. We also don't know if they have relieved the wench—er, the woman—of the parchment you seek, so we can allow none to escape should one of them be carrying it."

Arcanus nodded, recognising that his part of the plan would be to provide the distraction. Aye, he could do that well enough, especially with the aid of magyck.

With a wink at Berik, he started the incantation while pulling materials out of his spell pouch: some copper coins, a pinch of elderflower root, and a hefty dash of hot chili pepper seed.

Aerem recontartem, vini teneskar,
Reveal thy wealth and unveil thy shimmer
Riches beyond counting, untold gold,
Now flow for me, I beg thee,
But do not forget, the hex created,
An allergic reaction to blow noses off faces...

As Arcanus performed the spell, he placed the coins on the ground and circled them with both the elderflower and pepper powders. A major sneeze began building up, and he quickly pinched his nose shut to avoid drawing attention before he was ready.

The spell wouldn't truly hurt anyone, but it would keep them distracted long enough for Berik to knock them out—ensuring they could safely rescue the woman and the skrol.

"Radical Candor is about caring personally and challenging directly, not about winning or losing."

"When bosses are too invested in everyone getting along, they avoid challenging directly."

"The goal is to be clear and kind at the same time."

"Radical Candor builds trust and opens the door for the kind of communication that helps you achieve the results you are aiming for."

"It is your job to provide guidance, which involves a mix of praise and criticism, delivered to produce better results and help the other person grow."

— Kim Scott, Radical Candor

A golden shimmer began to form in place of the copper coins, multiplying in number until they created a sizeable pile—enough to attract the attention of any greedy observers. Once the gold coins had fully materialised, it was time to call attention to Arcanus's woes.

Producing a sizeable sack, he quickly tore a rip down the side, making it appear as though his precious coins had spilled all over the ground. With a few whispered words, he cast a spell ensuring that none but those inside the storehouse would hear or see what was about to unfold.

Now, for the big act.

The storehouse's weathered reddish-brown bricks and steel beams gleamed under the morning sun. Its pointed roof, reminiscent of Arcanus's favourite hat, was covered in small copper vents and chimneys, occasionally releasing wisps of steam into the air.

The door—made of brass—was covered in etched panels, its once-elegant design dulled by time. Above it, a cracked clock ticked away, its hands driven by a small army of spinning cogs.

Enough sightseeing.

Clearing his throat, Arcanus raised a dramatic hand to his eyes and let it go.

A loud, wretched wail echoed through the alley. Over and over, between fake burping and belching, he blubbered over his spilled coins, careful not to glance toward the storehouse. Any moment now.

Right on cue, several mercenaries poured out of the doorway, shielding their eyes against the glaring morning sun.

They'd see what he wanted them to see.

An old, drunk man bemoaning his lost fortune—an easy

mark for mercs who would skin their own grandmothers for a copper.

Once their eyes adjusted, they began grinning and whispering among themselves.

Evil bastards.

"Hey, old one! What's yer caterwauling fer? Disturbin' the peace o' good folk here."

"Yeah, I'm sure, asshole," Arcanus muttered under his breath, too low for them to hear.

He stumbled a little, fell to his knees, and slowly began gathering the coins, stuffing them clumsily back into the torn sack.

The group advanced, their intentions clear.

Arcanus looked up with bleary, rheumy eyes and smiled at them, playing the role of the helpless fool.

"Aye, lads. Will ye be helpin' an old man collect his hard-earned winnings?"

They laughed nastily before one of them stomped on his fingers.

Damn, that hurt!

Arcanus had to bite his cheek to keep from swearing aloud.

"Sure, ol' timer. We be helpin' ye—GET A MOVE ON! This here gold is ours now."

One of them kicked him aside while the others swarmed the ground like flesh-eating bugs, stuffing the illusory gold into their pockets. Try as they might, while their pouches bulged with gold, there was always more left on the ground.

Then, the chili pepper powder took effect.

Sneezing erupted among them—loud, relentless sneezes. Their noses ran, their eyes blurred, and a deep, hacking cough spread through the group. It wasn't enough to stop them, but blinded by greed and their own affliction, they failed to notice the massive shadow looming behind them.

Whack! Whack! Whack! Whack! Whack!

Berik struck with brutal efficiency, knocking each one unconscious before dragging them over to a nearby tree and tying them down. They wouldn't be going anywhere anytime soon.

Stealthily, they crept toward the storehouse door. Arcanus leaned down, peering through the keyhole—but he couldn't see a damn thing.

"What now? Do we just burst in and take the rest by surprise?" he whispered, leaning back against the wall.

Berik's eyes never left the window. "Do you have a temporary sleep spell?" he whispered.

"Sure."

"Can you take them down without going in?" Berik asked, his tone dubious.

Arcanus snorted and tugged his hat firmly onto his head. "Course I can. I was a prodigy at spells…"

Stars above, earth below,
Let peaceful rest now fill these souls.
By the sun's glow and daylight's grace,
Fall thine occupants into sleep's embrace.

Berik raised a brow, and Arcanus answered crossly, "Give it a minute!"

Soon enough, they heard the familiar thudding of bodies hitting the floor. A minute later, all was quiet—it was time to make their entrance.

Berik cautiously opened the door and stepped in first, signalling for Arcanus to follow.

The storehouse smelled of oil and aged wood. Its walls and floors were made of polished planks that had likely gleamed with care once upon a time, but now stood abandoned and dusty. Hanging from the rafters were several sets of pulley systems and chains, useful for lifting heavy goods. A small office corner had been created using a wall of frosted glass panels, and a messy desk covered in old blueprints sat gathering dust. In the left corner, a steam-powered heater chugged along quietly, keeping the office warm and cosy despite the storehouse's apparent abandonment.

Stepping over snoring bodies, they scanned the room for the woman—the Lamia who had stolen the bloody parchment.

"Berik, check if any of these guys have the parchment on them. I'll find the woman."

Berik nodded and started going through pockets, taking care to tie each mercenary up after the search. Meanwhile, Arcanus searched the dusty storeroom, which held little save for old, empty wooden barrels and a few broken chairs. Then, he noticed a small staircase leading to a second floor.

Moving carefully, he ascended the steps, treading lightly. There was a door at the top, and with a deep breath, he opened it—hoping he wouldn't find something that would make him hurl.

He wasn't squeamish, but he disliked unpleasant surprises with a passion.

There, lying on the floor as though she had not a care in the world, was a dark-haired woman.

She stretched a good way across the floor—taller than the average woman. Arcanus turned her face toward him and took in her features. Strong brows framed elfin features and dusky skin. Her hands were callused and strong, yet still unmistakably feminine. There was a stubborn set to her brow that made him groan—he could already tell Berik and the woman would fight.

Hoisting her over his shoulder—and wheezing slightly at the effort because, yes, she was tall and bloody heavy—Arcanus carried her downstairs and placed her upright on a chair.

Berik had secured the remaining mercs, and at Arcanus's questioning look, he shook his head.

"Drats. Does this mean it's still on her? Did she lose it?" Arcanus muttered.

"Why don't you wake her, and we can see—unless you want to check her yourself?" Berik grumbled.

"I'll wake her. I have no intention of hearing that I accosted someone in their sleep," Arcanus replied dryly.

Holding a bottle of smelling salts under her nose, he waited.

After a few moments, her nose twitched, and her eyes shot open. She was about to scream but decided against it—and headbutted him instead.

A muffled laugh came from Berik as Arcanus grunted, staggering back. The woman moved as if to get up, but Berik stepped forward, towering over her and pointing the end of his axe at her throat.

She reached for her side and grunted, realising that the mercenaries had stripped her of her weapons when they captured her. Raising her hands in a gesture of temporary truce, she glared at Berik.

"Who are you?" Berik barked.

"What's it to ye, stranger?" she shot back.

"Since we rescued you, the least you owe us is your name," Arcanus groaned, rubbing his poor, abused head.

"Aye, ye did, Sorcerer, but it took ye long enough…" she huffed.

Berik's eyes bulged. "Are you complaining that we were late to rescue you?? It was by chance that we found your bloody bracelet!"

"Nay, Smithy. I talk te the Sorcerer. He has been chasin' me a while now. My name is Sorche. Sorcerer, what's yours?"

From there, it all went downhill.

Arcanus could see neither trusted the other. There were plenty of misunderstandings between them, and they each blamed the other for everything—from bad weather to finding a hole in the money pouch.

"Sorche, Berik, please—no more arguing. You've been going at it for twenty minutes, and this is going nowhere," Arcanus sighed, pinching the bridge of his nose.

"Sorche, we came after you for the Skrol. It's urgent I find it and return it to the Academy. Do you have it on you?"

Sorche shook her head. "The one bastard left a couple of nights ago after receiving a missive from Darsura, the mountain stronghold. I'm sorry, but he's taken it to Rafe."

Berik's eyes bulged again, and he lunged for her.

Sorche barely ducked out of the way.

"ENOUGH, Berik! Contain yourself!" Arcanus snapped.

Then, turning back to Sorche, he demanded, "Why did you leave us clues to follow you if the Skrol was no longer in your possession?"

"It's obvious, isn't it? She needed us to get her out of this jam since she couldn't do it herself," Berik snarled.

"Is that true?" Arcanus asked.

Sorche nodded. "I need you to get me free. My sister is being held by Rafe, and I knew you would come after me if you believed the Skrol was still here. I had to get free—for her. And I will be accompanying you to Darsura."

"HELL NO!" bellowed Berik.

Arcanus nodded, holding up a hand to calm him. He understood her reasoning, but now what?

It was obvious they were all heading in the same direction, and these two clearly couldn't stand each other.

He needed clarity, and that started with asking the right questions.

"Since we'll be traveling together, we need some questions answered—to get to the bottom of the aggro you're both carrying…"

At this, both Sorche and Berik fell silent and tense, folding their arms across their chests like a pair of angry birds.

"Guys, we aren't going anywhere until we get this straightened out, and time is of the essence. Who wants to go first?"

Sorche spoke first, voice clipped.

"He's been chasing me for a while now, and I had no idea why. It's very frustrating being unable to perform your job when you have a hulking shadow following you everywhere!"

Berik was about to snap back when Arcanus raised a hand.

"Understood. He made things difficult for you. Berik, go ahead."

Berik's jaw tightened. "The men who were chasing you killed my family and burned my village down."

Sorche's expression shifted—for a moment, she looked aghast.

"I'm indeed sorry, Smithy. I had no idea they had done that. That is a terrible tragedy. My condolences."

No one spoke for several minutes as the weight of the words settled.

An Academy lesson Arcanus had learned early on resurfaced:

Effective communication is built on verifying information and ensuring the message is clear and precise.

"Now that we've said our pieces, and while they were harsh truths, candor is always the best option," he said firmly.

"We avoid fabrications, misinterpretations, and assumptions. The politics of life are tricky and messy, so we need to anticipate others' reactions, understand motivations, and plan ahead.

"We must remain proactive, act above reproach, and carry ourselves with integrity. Never give anyone the chance to question your strength of character."

> "Seek first to understand, then to be understood."
>
> "Most people do not listen with the intent to understand; they listen with the intent to reply."
>
> "Be a light, not a judge. Be a model, not a critic."
>
> — Stephen R. Covey, The 7 Habits of Highly Effective People

> "Great leaders do not try to please everyone."
>
> "Leaders who set out to give are more productive than leaders who seek to get."
>
> "Initiating is really and truly difficult, and that is what leaders do. They see something others are ignoring, and they jump on it."
>
> — Seth Godin, Tribes

Arcanus looked at both of them and waved a hand. "Let's get out of here. I need food and rest after today. We can return to the inn for the night and set off early tomorrow morning. We'll sneak in and take the rear staircase in case those mercs come looking for Sorche. Dinner and a meeting in my room tonight, okay?"

Both nodded, and they set off to gather their horses.

Sorche had no horse, so they doubled up on Arcanus's—it

was a short ride back to the inn, and his horse could carry both of them that far without strain.

Arcanus sent Berik ahead to scout the stables and check for any lurking mercenaries. Thankfully, the coast was clear. After instructing the stable boy to look after their horses for another night, they headed for the back entrance of the inn.

Again, Berik went ahead first, making sure all was safe before signalling for them to follow. Arcanus chatted lightly with Sorche as they waited, then made their way inside once Berik gave the all-clear.

Berik had procured a room for Sorche, and they each set about washing and changing before mealtime. The innkeeper, well-versed in their habits, left loaded trays outside Arcanus's door. He fetched them and began setting out dinner for everyone.

As Arcanus glanced around the pleasant room, he felt a wave of relief at being in comfort once more.

The steam heater puffed away merrily in the corner, adding to the cosy atmosphere. The polished steam lamps were adorned with delicate green leaves, casting a warm glow across the glistening walnut floors. The grand bed, with its wonderfully plush mattress, called to his tired muscles.

His body must have sighed unconsciously, because when he looked up, both Berik and Sorche were glaring at him with mulish expressions.

Their stubbornness reminded him of a bunch of villagers he'd helped a while back.

EDICTS OF THE WISE

Clear Communication is Non-Negotiable

Clarity in communication isn't optional—it's essential. Say what you mean and mean what you say. Vague words lead to confusion. There's no value in dressing up messages to sound nicer or more agreeable. When you're clear and direct, you build trust, eliminate uncertainty, and create room for meaningful conversations. Don't leave people guessing—make your words work for you, not against you.

Integrity in communication is everything. Words should never be twisted, manipulated, or used as tools for self-interest. Honest leadership means speaking with sincerity, not manoeuvring conversations for personal gain. People see through manipulation. It may work in the short term, but in the long run, it erodes credibility. Say what needs to be said—truthfully, directly, and respectfully—and let the results follow.

Authenticity isn't a buzzword; it's the foundation of leadership. Being real means being consistent, truthful, and acting with purpose. It doesn't mean being blunt for the sake of it or oversharing without thought. Great leaders don't craft a persona; they show up as they are. Speak with honesty, own your perspective, and ensure your words align with your actions. People follow leaders they trust, not those who perform for approval.

Candor Creates Stronger Teams

There are four ways to approach feedback, but only one leads to success. Radical Candor—challenging directly while caring personally—is the gold standard. The other three approaches destroy teams. Ruinous Empathy avoids hard truths, leading to long-term failure. Manipulative Insincerity serves only personal agendas and corrodes trust. Obnoxious Aggression may get attention but crushes morale. The best teams operate with Radical Candor—direct, honest, and caring conversations that drive real results.

Communication is a two-way responsibility. You control what you say, how you say it, and how you follow up. Before assuming a misunderstanding is someone else's fault, ask yourself: Was I clear? Did I confirm alignment? Did I make sure my message landed? Only when you've done everything in your power can you fairly question whether the issue lies with the other person. Leadership means owning communication—not blaming gaps on others.

Misunderstandings don't happen out of nowhere. They happen when something was unclear, lost in translation, or avoided altogether. If a message doesn't land, assume first that the delivery was flawed. Go back, clarify, and ensure alignment. Blaming others for not understanding is lazy. Strong leaders reinforce and refine their message until it's understood.

Candor isn't cruel, it's kind. Being clear and direct is an act of respect. Avoiding hard conversations, sugarcoating, or hiding behind politeness creates misalignment, inefficiency, and wasted effort. But candor also isn't about being harsh, some mistake "brutal honesty" for effectiveness, but cruelty disguised as truth is still cruelty. The goal isn't to be sharp, it's to be clear, constructive, and actionable.

Clarity Drives Success—Ask the Right Questions

Uncertainty isn't an excuse for inaction. If something is unclear, ask. Too many people hesitate because they fear looking uninformed, but making assumptions leads to bigger mistakes. Clarity is a choice. If you don't know—ask. If something doesn't make sense—challenge it. There's no shame in seeking understanding; the only real mistake is pretending you know when you don't.

Social norms and unspoken rules exist everywhere, but that doesn't mean they should go unchallenged. If something seems ambiguous—clarify it. If an assumption is at play—verify it. A simple question costs nothing. A misunderstanding costs time, effort, and credibility. Choose the question.

Assumptions lead to failure. When you assume without verifying, you open the door to misalignment, confusion, and frustration. It's far better to pause and confirm than to assume and regret. Effective communication is built on verification, not presumption.

Take Full Ownership of Your Communication

At the end of the day, the only thing you can control is yourself—your words, your approach, your reactions. You can't control how others interpret your message, but you can control how clear, precise, and effective your delivery is. You can't force people to listen, but you can go further to create clarity early.

Taking ownership of communication eliminates excuses and drives real impact. Every word either creates alignment or causes confusion—choose wisely.

Clarity Creates Stronger Organisations

Clarity is the foundation of success. Whether it's setting expectations for a team, defining priorities, or shaping the future of a business, precise communication is everything. Ambiguity leads to frustration, inefficiency, and rework. Clear expectations create alignment, enable better decisions, and drive accountability.

If you don't define success, people will interpret it for themselves—and that's when problems start. The best leaders don't leave expectations open-ended. They make sure every action ties back to a clear, measurable goal.

Politics exist whether we like them or not. Ignoring the game doesn't mean you escape it, it just means you play it poorly. You don't need to be political in your approach, but you must be aware that others will be. Navigate with intention. Anticipate moves, understand motivations, and plan strategically. The best leaders don't get caught up in politics, but they also don't get blindsided by those who do.

Transparency Builds Trust

Transparency isn't optional. Waiting to see how things unfold, reacting only when forced, or staying silent in uncertainty is weak leadership. Strong leaders step forward, set the tone, and shape the message before it's shaped for them. Being first with the truth builds credibility. When challenges arise, people should turn to you for answers—not question your motives.

Visibility is power. If you don't control your message, someone else will. Strong leaders use visibility to build trust, set expectations, and drive alignment.

Lead with Strength and Integrity

Above all, lead with integrity. This isn't about being soft—it's about being strong enough to do the right thing, even when it's hard. Treat people with fairness, honesty, and respect. There will be moments when taking the high road costs you something in the short term—but integrity is a long game.

Being above reproach means never giving anyone a valid reason to question your character. Leadership isn't about winning every battle—it's about standing for something greater. And that means choosing clarity, honesty, and trust—even when it's not easy.

Build a Culture of Clarity and Candor

Coaching your team to be clear and direct isn't optional—it's a leadership responsibility. Clarity removes confusion. Candor eliminates hesitation. If people can't speak openly—if they second-guess whether they can say what needs to be said—you've already lost time and momentum. Encourage directness, model it yourself, and create an environment where honesty isn't a risk—it's the norm.

Culture is built by what we allow and what we reject. If you want a team that values directness, integrity, and open dialogue, you have to enforce those standards relentlessly. That means never settling for vagueness, tolerating politics, making excuses, or dishonesty.

Resilience and Focus Define Leadership

Resilience isn't about pretending things don't affect you. It's about understanding how they do—and choosing how you respond. Learn your own triggers. Know what fuels you and what drains you. Recognise how your energy impacts those around you.

Strong leaders don't suppress emotions—they master them. Resilience isn't just a personal skill—it's something you model and inspire in others. Teach your team to navigate setbacks, manage stress, and move forward with confidence.

Perspective is everything. Without the right focus, energy is wasted on things that don't move the needle. The best teams don't just work hard—they work on the right things. Anything else is wasted motion. And wasted motion is the enemy of progress.

Clarity Without Confidence Falls Flat

Clear words mean nothing if they're delivered with hesitation. If you water down your message, second-guess yourself, or over-explain, people will pick up on it. Confidence amplifies clarity. If you don't believe what you're saying, no one else will either. Own your words. Say them like they matter—because they do.

Avoiding Hard Conversations is Just Slow Failure

Dodging a tough conversation doesn't make the problem go away—it just lets it get bigger. Leaders who sugarcoat, sidestep, or delay tough discussions aren't being kind; they're setting their teams up for misalignment, resentment, and wasted time. If something needs to be said, say it now, say it clearly, and move forward. Clarity cuts through the noise. Avoidance just adds to it.

Side Quest
The Barn or the Mill?

The argument was coming from the edge of the village, where the villagers had gathered around a carpenter and a miller, both shouting over a half-finished barn.

"I need this barn done before the storms hit!" the carpenter barked, gesturing wildly at the beams. "We're out of lumber because someone decided to stockpile it for their mill!"

The miller crossed his arms. "And if the mill isn't running, the grain rots—storms or no storms! The lumber was promised to me first."

Arcanus raised his voice above the din. "Enough, gentlemen. We're here now—explain what's going on, and I might be able to assist."

The carpenter huffed. "We're rebuilding the barn for the coos (cows). But we're behind because he—" he jabbed a finger at the miller, "—took the lumber I requested."

"And you, miller?" Arcanus asked, turning to him.

"The storms ruined part of my mill's structure last spring. If it isn't repaired, the grain gets ruined, and we'll lose our food supply."

Arcanus nodded, considering their words. "Here's what I see: two problems, one resource, and no clear agreements. Did either of you define what you needed and when?"

Both men looked away, mumbling excuses.

He pressed on. "From now on, we fix that. When you request something, make it clear—how much, by when, and why. No assumptions. Clear requirements, understood by all."

Stepping closer, his voice remained firm but kind. "You also need to stop seeing each other as the enemy. People play games when there's uncertainty—so be transparent and plan ahead. Who will get the next shipment of lumber? Decide that together, now."

After a long pause, the carpenter spoke. "The mill gets the next shipment. But only if I get priority after that."

The miller nodded. "Agreed."

Arcanus smiled and nodded. "Good. Now, one more thing: do this with grace. Assume the best of each other and be above reproach. The storms may hit, but at least you'll weather them together."

As the villagers returned to work, the miller grumbled, "You handled that well, stranger."

Arcanus shrugged. "It's not about winning or losing—it's about clarity and care. If we care enough about others to be clear, even when it's hard, we'll weather the storms."

The miller grinned. "You sound like someone I've heard of—a grey-cloaked wanderer who always seemed to be two steps ahead."

Arcanus chuckled. "Perhaps. But he had the wisdom of years. Me? I'm just figuring it out as I go."

> *"The key to leadership is bravely going ahead without question and doing what is right!"*
>
> — Leela, Futurama, Season 2 Episode 2

After recalling that particular episode, Arcanus declared a truce between Berik and Sorche. They needed to work together, and like it or not, she was now a member of the team.

Unifying people who instantly hated one another was

yet another headache, but one he was determined to push through—for the sake of the world.

His thoughts drifted back to a time when Berik had managed to bring peace and unity between goblins. If he had accomplished that, then surely, he could do this.

Side Quest
The Trebuchet Dilemma

The golden sun dipped behind the mountains as the party stumbled upon a clearing. In the centre stood a crude wooden contraption—part trebuchet, part mystery. Around it, a group of mismatched engineers argued loudly, their voices bouncing off the rocks.

At the heart of the chaos was a wiry half-elf named Garvin, pacing furiously and muttering under his breath.

Arcanus paused, his staff tapping the ground softly. "What in the name of magic's fine print is this racket about?"

Garvin threw up his hands. "It's supposed to be a trebuchet, but nobody agrees on how to finish it! They're blaming each other, and I'm stuck trying to make sense of it all."

Berik stepped forward, his gaze sharp. "Enough. Everyone stop."

The engineers froze mid-shout, turning toward him like children caught stealing pies.

Berik's voice was calm, but there was steel beneath it. "One at a time. Speak clearly. What's the problem?"

A dwarf wiped grease from his hands and grumbled, "The counterweight's too heavy. It'll topple the whole thing."

"Nonsense," a gnome barked. "The release arm's angled wrong. It'll never fire far enough."

Berik listened patiently before turning to Garvin. "And you? What do you think is wrong?"

"I—uh," Garvin stammered. "I just want it to work! They keep arguing, and I don't know what to do."

Berik sighed and nodded to Arcanus, signalling for him to take over.

Arcanus stepped forward, happy to intervene when needed. "Garvin, you're leading this group. They need direction, not chaos. It's up to you to keep them focused and working toward the goal."

Garvin frowned, rubbing the back of his neck. "But what if I make the wrong decision?"

"Then you'll adjust," Arcanus said firmly. "It's not about being perfect. It's about keeping everyone moving forward. Be clear. Be honest. And always focus on what matters."

Under Berik's watchful eye, the engineers quieted.

Garvin began asking questions, listening carefully to their ideas. He weighed their concerns, gave each a chance to speak, and, with a steady voice, made the call: adjust the counterweight first, then tweak the release angle.

By nightfall, the trebuchet stood tall and ready—a proud testament to clarity and teamwork.

As they prepared to leave, Garvin approached them, looking sheepish. "Thanks for stepping in. I didn't realise how much my own confusion was holding them back."

"Confusion is natural," Arcanus replied. "But it's your job to cut through it, not add to it. Leadership isn't about being the loudest—it's about giving others a reason to trust you."

As the party headed back to the trail, one of the engineers

muttered, "That contraption better work. It looked like something that smeggin' Cat would have built."

Berik smirked. "If it doesn't, at least it'll make for a spectacular explosion."

With that, Sorche, Berik, and Arcanus vanished into the woods, the trebuchet—and Garvin's newfound confidence—standing tall in the clearing.

THE UNWRITTEN RULES

Sometimes people just want to share, not solve— listen first, ask before offering advice.

In social situations, not every conversation is a request for solutions. If a friend is venting about a tough day, they may not want advice—they may just want to feel heard. Instead of jumping in with fixes, try asking, *"Do you want advice, or do you just need to vent?"* This small shift helps build strong, trust-based relationships.

Tone and facial expressions can change how words are received—match words with intent.

Saying the right thing in a flat or serious tone can sometimes be misinterpreted as harsh. If you mean something in a positive or neutral way, a small adjustment in tone, expression, or body language can make a big difference. A slight smile, a softer voice, or adding *"I appreciate what you're doing"* before feedback can help others receive your message as intended.

Not Everyone Communicates the Way You Do— Adjust, But Know When to Step Up

People process and express thoughts differently. Some are highly verbal, while others need time to think before responding. If someone is quiet, it doesn't always mean they disagree or have nothing valuable to add—they may just be processing. But there are moments when staying silent is the wrong move. Leadership, teamwork, and influence sometimes require you to step forward, contribute, and make your voice heard. The key is knowing when to hold back and when to engage. Read the room, assess the moment, and choose wisely.

Timing Matters—Even the Right Words Can Fail in the Wrong Moment

There's a right time and place for every conversation. Offering feedback in the heat of the moment, raising an issue when someone is already overwhelmed, or jumping into a deep discussion when the mood is light can backfire. Social awareness is just as important as the message itself. Read the room, gauge the energy, and choose the right moment to ensure your words land effectively. If you want your message to stick, timing is everything.

THE MIRROR OF MASTERY

» How can I balance directness with emotional awareness in my communication, ensuring clarity without unintentionally causing discomfort or resistance?

» When has my intent been different from the way my message was received, and what patterns can I recognise in these situations?

» In what situations do I find it hardest to be candid, and what underlying fears or assumptions might be holding me back?

CHAPTER 5

The Compass of Judicious Discernment

Main Quest
The Odyssey of Purposeful Leadership

The sun shone brightly as the party left the inn. Each traveller, having eaten a good breakfast and looking well-rested, set off in hopeful spirits. Arcanus led the way, with Sorche following, and Berik bringing up the rear—keeping watch on Sorche, of all things.

Arcanus had insisted that she have a horse of her own, but Berik remained stubbornly paranoid.

It was one thing to be careful, to be watchful, to be prepared. It was an entirely different beast when a traveling team member was treated as a spy—or worse, a potential enemy.

Beyond these teething issues, which constantly tested his leadership skills, Arcanus was also dealing with an unforgiving rash. His decision to continue wearing his formal wizard's hat was a personal one—it had been a gift from the High Elder, and he would not part with it during his waking hours.

Blast and curse this rash and the sweats!

Scratching at his head, then righting the hat once more, he was too preoccupied to notice that Berik had stopped, holding up an arm to signal the group to halt.

Sorche frowned at Arcanus, but he remained distracted—until he finally heard it.

Singing.

Startled that someone was on their path, he turned to see both Berik and Sorche staring at him in bemusement.

Pretty good singing, too, accompanied by a lute of some variety.

Berik lifted a brow—an unspoken question. What do you want to do?

Arcanus held up his palm, signalling they should wait for the singer to reveal themselves.

Berik nodded in agreement, then turned to Sorche, who moved her horse behind his, watching their rear while he remained in a relaxed but watchful stance atop his mount.

A moment later, a slim, short fellow with muddy brown hair, one green eye, one blue, and a ton of freckles stepped onto their path mid-song. His extremely long ears, which reminded Arcanus of a mule, twitched as he took in the group before him.

He stopped awkwardly, then smiled and took a deep bow.

"Good morrow, sirs and lady! I am Juju, head bard to the Elder Wizard of Loria, seeking fabulous adventures for my new show. I bid you welcome!"

Berik and Sorche exchanged a glance—both immediately aware that the elf bard had just lied.

Had he truly been associated with the Elder of Loria, Arcanus would have mentioned such a character before now.

They grinned at one another, then turned to observe Arcanus's startled expression.

"Indeed, Bard. You must be one of the greats to entertain such high company," Arcanus said, recovering his composure behind a polite smile.

Juju, believing they had bought his story, nodded and began walking alongside Arcanus's horse as the party resumed their journey.

"Yes, my good man! I have seen things that would turn you green with envy or, possibly, frighten you to death. But, being in this business, I often undertake perilous journeys in search of new material, as the Elder is a demanding audience who entertains nobility from every corner of the continent.

"I say—that is a fabulous hat! Where'd you get it? Also, did you know you have an enormous rash on your skull and neck? Terrible thing, rashes. Especially in this hot weather."

Arcanus nodded and smiled again, fully aware of the Elder's routines—after all, he had occasionally managed them himself before departing on this mission.

Juju continued talking for the next hour, seemingly unaware that he was being sized up by the rest of the group.

Arcanus glanced at Berik, who rolled his eyes and shook his head—clearly disapproving of the additional weight.

No surprise there.

Turning to Sorche, Arcanus saw her flash him a grin and a thumbs-up, which earned another eyeroll from Berik.

Deciding to deep listen to Juju, Arcanus cast a glamour on himself.

To Juju, he appeared his usual self—riding along, smiling—while Arcanus dived into the bard's conscience and memories.

As the team's leader and a wizard, he was the only one who could accurately discern whether someone was inherently good or not—aura reading was a handy skill, especially when one didn't have weeks to get to know a person.

Closing his eyes, he focused on Juju's presence.

The bard's aura appeared at first as a blurry swirl of bright yellow tinged with blue.

Then it came into focus.

It danced and flickered within him, like a flash of light in a container.

Juju, for all his extravagantly tall tales, was simply another soul trying to make his way in the world.

His aura was a mixture of enthusiastic cheekiness tinged with sadness—but Arcanus sensed no malice or cruelty.

He was glad they had come across him.

Perhaps Juju was exactly what the group needed to truly gel together before they faced what could very well be the end of times.

"So, what do you think?" Juju asked brightly, popping the cork on a familiar-looking bottle.

"Err—come again?" Arcanus stammered, blushing brilliant red at being caught unawares.

"Of me joining you fine folk for a wee spell, of course!" Juju grinned.

"I'll pay my own way, but I think it's better if I travel with a group of people instead of hotfooting it around alone. I'm a good judge of character. And I sense that you're good folk.

"Besides, seeing your large friend back there armed with several axes and who knows what else, I'd wager you've seen your fair share of adventures.

"I'd be very grateful if I could tag along for a bit—if that's okay with you?"

Juju took another whiff of the bottle and gagged, turning a brilliant shade of puce.

"Whew! What is this?! Smells like the bottom of a bog that's never been flushed!"

Berik snorted in disgust, and Arcanus gave him an amused smile.

He knew exactly what was annoying him.

"Sure, we'd be happy to have such a fine musician join us on our travels," Arcanus replied smoothly—smiling in secret amusement as Berik stiffened.

Berik was such an easy mark—it hardly seemed fair!

"Excellent! Here, catch!"

Juju tossed him the stinky bottle.

"Hey! Where'd you find this?!" Arcanus yelped in surprise.

"Took it from your pocket while you were looking at your friends." Juju smirked.

Berik looked like he wanted to strangle him.

As Juju walked ahead, lute in hand, Berik rode up alongside Arcanus.

"Why on earth are you letting him join us?" Berik growled.

Arcanus shrugged, nonchalant.

"I think we make a more wholesome foursome than a tense threesome, to be honest."

Berik's eyes widened in abject horror.

Sorche let out a hysterical giggle.

And so, Juju the bard became the party's newest member.

"The higher you go, the less likely your decisions will receive unanimous approval."

"Not everyone is going to like you."

"Prioritising speed over accuracy improves every decision." (But not too fast either.)

— Martin G. Moore, No Bullsh!t Leadership

"You are accountable for the success of a project, but the business has to own it."

"As a CIO, you are the first to step into traffic, to stand alone during a period of change before people come on board. That takes personal courage."

"Because IT people can see so much, it is their responsibility to influence investment priorities, not just execute on priorities set by internal business partners."

— Martha Heller, The CIO Paradox

A few hours later, the group came across several buildings—the early foundation of a new village. Spotting an inn-in-progress, they made their way toward The Cog and Nuts, a barely-put-together establishment that would serve as their resting place for the night.

Arcanus managed to secure four rooms and was relieved they wouldn't have to share, especially after that disagreement.

Heading back out to the inn's stables, he informed the others of their room assignments before instructing the stable boy to properly groom, water, and feed their horses. After offering his horse a final pat, he turned toward the inn, crossing his fingers for a quiet night.

The inn's brass fixtures, metallic beams, and copper roof made for an impressive sight despite its incomplete state. Above the entrance rested a shiny, well-designed cog surrounded by several nuts.

As far as signage went, this one was well done.

It sparked a sliver of hope that their rooms would be, at the very least, decent, despite the unfinished state of the village.

The main area—both lounge and dining space—was large, designed to house at least fifteen tables. Brass pipes crept shyly along the walls and ceilings in intricate patterns, making it clear that the inn not only provided hot water directly to each room, but also that each room had its own private bathroom.

A luxury for a barely-there village, but Arcanus wasn't about to complain.

The inn's walls were decorated in fine, dark oak interspersed with metalwork—craftsmanship that spoke of an experienced hand.

The pub area within was already decently stocked, boasting several mechanical ale pumps connected to taps that emerged from behind the counter.

Arcanus admired the design, wondering if the basement below played a role.

It would make sense if the ale pumps were connected to drums in the basement, keeping them out of sight while providing a constant, uninterrupted flow.

He glanced around the room and noted that his comrades had disappeared.

Assuming they had headed to their rooms, he made his way to his own.

The rooms were large and airy, featuring bright copper-framed beds, soft-looking mattresses, small wind-up clocks, several brass lamps, and a heating unit.

A quick glance into the bathroom revealed a deep tub, a copper and oak vanity table, and an indoor toilet.

All in all, a very comfortable space, with amenities that would please anyone.

Deciding to settle in, Arcanus prepared for a soothing soak, allowing the warm water to ease his tired body and act as a balm for his weary soul.

After three days, Juju had firmly ingrained himself within the group. Polite, funny, salty as hell, and always ready with a sharp retort, he had proven himself more than just an entertainer.

At the moment, he was deep into one of his favourite songs—something he called "Song of Rest," though the lyrics seemed to change as often as he bathed.

Not too often, but enough to notice.

Draw near, brave travellers ye,
And listen to a story of heroes (so I've been told...).
A trio strange with quirks and more,
Who've brought mayhem to every door...
Berik's face darkens dramatically.
First is the warrior, big and sulky,
Face like thunder, always brooding.
Swings his sword with a dramatic wail,
"Why must I fight? Oh, -"

Just as Berik was about to hop off his horse and pummel Juju, the bard let out a great shout:

"NOVIA! We've arrived! Hooray! I can't wait to play my new songs for an audience!"

The group picked up the pace, approaching the city's grand gates where they were met by a representative of Wizard Marmaduke.

The man—a gaunt fellow with a long, spindly nose and sallow skin—stepped forward and addressed them with practiced formality.

"Welcome, Wizard Arcanus, gentlemen, and lady. The Wizard Marmaduke bids his friend, Arcanus, come visit for a spell. The rest of you may seek shelter at the inn and enjoy all the city has to offer."

Arcanus nodded at the group, arranging their stay at a beautifully quaint copper inn surrounded by a man-made moat, complete with ducks and swans.

He delegated the care of their horses to Berik, reminding him to give them a thorough grooming and double their feed.

After ensuring everyone had their accommodations settled, Arcanus turned back to the waiting representative.

"Lead the way, my good man."

The gaunt fellow bowed deeply before gliding forward, leading the way across cobblestone paths toward a magnificent castle.

Magnificent felt like an understatement.

The architecture and artistry unfolding before Arcanus's eyes were nothing short of breathtaking.

The castle's towers rose in sweeping arcs of bronze and iron, with clockwork gears visible along the exterior walls. Embedded within the metallic surfaces were blue and green gems, their facets catching the sunlight and scattering bursts of colour into the air.

The drawbridge itself was a masterpiece—crafted from interlocking obsidian pieces edged in gold, adorned with topaz gemstones that glowed like embers in the daylight.

Giant gears and cogs jutted from the castle's outer walls, encrusted with Citrine and garnet, creating a showstopping display of gemstone-studded teeth that pulsed with a golden-amber light when the mechanisms began to turn.

Steam vents, rimmed in moonstone, added an elegant, almost mystical quality, their vapor rising in gentle plumes into the sky.

They approached a massive set of oak doors interwoven with intricate metalwork, the craftsmanship so delicate it almost appeared magyk-infused.

Arcanus was almost certain that the castle had been partially constructed with the aid of magycks.

"Bad decisions made with good intentions are still bad decisions."

> *"You absolutely cannot make a series of good decisions without first confronting the brutal facts."*
> — Jim Collins, How the Mighty Fall: And Why Some Companies Never Give In, and Good to Great: Why Some Companies Make the Leap...And Others Don't

> *"I do not need to do more smart things. I just need to do fewer dumb things. I need to avoid making emotional decisions and swinging at bad pitches. I need to think!"*
>
> *"Emotional decisions lead to costly mistakes."*
>
> *"Learn from the failures of others to avoid making the same mistakes."*
> — Keith J. Cunningham, The Road Less Stupid

Within the castle, the great hall was illuminated by an amethyst crystal chandelier, its light refracted through exquisitely spinning clockwork fans that diffused the glow across the room. The walls were adorned with polished oak panels, inset with semi-precious stone mosaics showcasing mechanical wonders and starry skies. The onyx-tiled floors gleamed underfoot, their surfaces rimmed with thin gold veins.

The throne room was a display of riches. The throne itself was a masterpiece of platinum and steel, twisted together like vines and embedded with diamonds, peridots, and topaz. Behind it stood a giant, operational clock face, its numbers crafted from black diamonds, its hands tipped with aquamarine studs.

The Ruler of Novia, Nutella Juggernaut, greeted Arcanus warmly and bid him to be seated at his left side.

Before Arcanus could move, a booming voice filled the hall. "ARCANUS!"

The Wizard Marmaduke had arrived—a wide grin stretched across his face.

Arcanus turned, breaking into a broad smile.

"Marmaduke, you old goat! It's been too long!"

They embraced before taking their seats.

Arcanus studied his old friend. The large, dusky-skinned man had gained quite a bit of weight around his middle—life must have been comfortable here.

His thick hair and beard, now greying, were as wild as ever, and Arcanus felt a pang of envy as he rubbed his shiny, slightly rash-ridden dome.

Despite his relaxed appearance, Marmaduke's liquid silver eyes remained sharp—missing nothing.

His wizard's robes—a matte black fabric that was cool to the touch—flowed with an unnatural grace, as if alive with magyck.

Nutella excused himself, leaving Arcanus and Marmaduke alone.

For a while, they sat in companionable silence.

Arcanus raised a quizzical brow at his friend, who sat opposite him in an almost comical pose—legs unfurled and crossed at the ankles, fingers steepled across his not-so-respectable belly, a peaceful look on his face.

Marmaduke appeared to be in his own world.

"Seems like you have a wonderful setup here, Marmaduke…" Arcanus chided, waiting for him to open up.

Marmaduke sighed, his relaxed demeanour slipping.

"I do, but we're having trouble…"

Arcanus straightened, angling his chair toward him.

"What do you mean?"

Marmaduke exhaled heavily and sat up, rubbing his beard in frustration.

"We've been dealing with a string of expensive thefts—getting bolder by the month. I've personally questioned guards and workers alike, but I haven't gained any ground.

"I do know where it's heading, though—one of my spies relayed this information to us several days ago."

He frowned, his large hand stroking his beard.

Arcanus narrowed his eyes. "What's the target? Same thing every time?"

Marmaduke nodded grimly. "It's a very rare metal, and you know it well. We use it in our alchemical spells…"

Arcanus's stomach dropped.

"You don't mean—"

"I do."

Arcanus groaned. "Oh no. Mercin."

Mercury and tin combined.

Marmaduke let out a frustrated sigh and ran a hand across his face.

Arcanus's expression darkened. "I bet I know where it's gone."

Marmaduke leaned forward. "What do you mean?"

"It's gone to Darsura, hasn't it?" Arcanus asked.

Marmaduke's silver eyes widened. "Yes—but how did you know?"

Arcanus ignored the question. "Never mind that. You need to stop mining the mineral for now."

Marmaduke frowned. "I don't understand. What's going on?"

Arcanus shook his head. "I can't tell you everything at this stage, but I'm on a mission for the High Elder, and this ties into it. I need you to trust me. You must shut the mines down—at least for now."

Marmaduke scoffed. "Arcanus, while you and I practice magyck, this city operates using logic and the rule of law.

"I cannot order the council to shut down the mines—it's one of our primary exports and our largest source of revenue.

"The council would have my hide!"

Arcanus sat in deep thought, but before he could respond, Marmaduke jumped to his feet and began pacing.

"If you could just tell me why—"

Arcanus shook his head.

"I cannot, my friend. I would if I could, but I cannot at this moment."

Marmaduke exhaled sharply. "Then what do you suggest?"

"When does the council meet again?"

Marmaduke rubbed his temples. "This afternoon. It's the annual summit, so everyone who needs to be there will be."

Arcanus's jaw tightened. "Can you get me in? I must convince them to shut the mines down—at least until my mission is complete."

Marmaduke hesitated, then nodded.

They would go their separate ways for now. But before the day was through, they would stand before the council.

Several hours later

Arcanus was told to wait outside a massive chamber upon his arrival. As he stood there, he could hear murmurs, scattered applause, and the occasional sharp remark.

After a few minutes, the door opened, and Marmaduke stuck his head out, nodding.

Without a word, Arcanus stepped inside, quietly taking the nearest available seat.

The room was breathtaking—its walls a cool, mother-of-pearl shade that seemed to shimmer in the light. A massive round table, its surface adorned with intricate inlaid metalwork, took centre stage.

The chamber was filled with all the important delegates of the city, their voices overlapping as they argued, debated, and attempted to impress their points upon the rest of the attendees.

Along the sides of the room, several refreshment carts stood ready, offering a selection of beverages and pastries.

Not a substantial meal, but enough for those enduring long and tedious meetings to tide over their gnawing hunger.

After twenty minutes of tense deliberations, the chairwoman finally announced a break, and the delegates flocked to the refreshments.

Arcanus spotted Marmaduke speaking with the chairwoman.

She smiled, then nodded.

Marmaduke's own easy smile followed before he turned and headed toward Arcanus.

"She's given you my spot, directly after the break," he murmured, casually helping himself to a slice of cake.

Arcanus nodded, pouring them both a cup of tea.

This meeting was critical. He needed to secure the council's agreement before leaving the city.

And, come to think of it, he really wanted to see the fabled Lagoon City before departing. He hoped he would get the chance.

Fifteen minutes later, a delicate chime signalled the end of the break.

The delegates resumed their seats, ready for the next speaker.

To their surprise, it was not the one listed on the official agenda.

A visitor had taken the floor.

Arcanus rose to his feet, casting an amplification spell so that his voice would carry throughout the enormous chamber.

"Ladies and gentlemen, thank you for allowing me the opportunity to speak. I bring an important matter to the table—one which must be dealt with immediately."

His gaze swept across the room, locking onto several delegates.

Establish connection first. Make them listen.

"I understand that Marmaduke was meant to present the issue of the stolen Mercin today," he continued.

A ripple of gasps spread throughout the room.

Whispers erupted as delegates turned to one another, murmuring in alarm.

Arcanus let them speak—for a moment—before pressing forward.

"I was made aware of this issue as I am the official representative of the High Elder, and we are the largest buyers of this valuable metal.

"It brings me no pleasure to deliver bad news, but the mining and processing of Mercin must halt until we deal with the outside source stealing the metal."

An angry buzz filled the chamber as several delegates loudly voiced their disapproval.

The Master of Economics pushed himself to his feet, slamming his fist on the table.

"Absolutely not! This is our primary export—our biggest source of revenue!

Who knows how long it will take to hunt out this 'supposed' thief?!"

Arcanus raised a calm but commanding hand for silence.

"Ladies and gentlemen, this is not a vote.

You will not get to decide whether or not the mines continue operations.

Unfortunately for you, this decision is mine and mine alone."

A hush fell over the room.

"I will inform the High Elder today, and they will send missives across the continent—stating that the supply of Mercin will be halted until the threat is neutralised.

"I do not have to remind you that enough Mercin in the wrong hands can wipe out every living thing on this continent.

"Do you want to be responsible for such a fate?"

A heavy silence fell over the room.

Arcanus let it settle.

Then, with a finality that left no room for argument, he delivered his verdict:

"Mining and operations cease today.

All supplies will be placed on lockdown until further notice.

Any complaints may be filed with the Elder Council of Loria.

Thank you for your time."

He bowed, and together with Marmaduke, exited the chamber—leaving the cacophony of outraged voices behind.

As they strode through the halls, Marmaduke let out a lazy grin, tugging at his beard.

"You had to be an asshole about it, eh?" he mused.

"They're gonna hate you, even though you've probably saved their miserable lives."

Arcanus exhaled.

He felt bad about the white lie, but both he and Marmaduke knew it had been necessary.

With a warrior's grip, Arcanus clasped Marmaduke's forearm in thanks.

Marmaduke returned the grip, clapping him on the shoulder.

No words were needed between close friends.

The two headed for the nearest pub, in search of a fortifying ale to quench their thirst—and their spirits.

For now, disaster had been averted.

But for how long?

EDICTS OF THE WISE

Decisiveness is a Leadership Skill—Develop It

Decisiveness isn't about being reckless or impulsive. It's about knowing when to move fast and when to hold back. Some leaders rush into decisions without enough information. Others hesitate too long, letting opportunities pass them by. Both are mistakes.

The truth is speed often matters more than accuracy. A quick decision, adjusted later, is usually more effective than one delayed by endless analysis. Momentum drives success. If you hesitate too long, you fall behind. But don't mistake speed for carelessness—great decisions come from experience, instinct, and focusing on the right information when it truly matters.

If You Don't Have the Information, Go Get It

Sitting back and waiting for answers isn't leadership—it's passivity. Great leaders are proactive. They ask questions, challenge assumptions, and seek out the right people to fill knowledge gaps. The worst decisions don't come from a lack of information—they come from failing to look for it.

But there's a limit. Endless data collection leads to paralysis. At some point, you'll have enough to make the call. That's when decisiveness kicks in. Act. Move forward. Own the outcome.

When It's Your Call, Make It

Leadership isn't about waiting for universal agreement. If you're the one responsible, it's on you to decide. A leader who refuses to make decisions is a leader who fails. Decisions create movement. Movement drives teams forward.

It's easy to worry about getting it wrong. It's easy to hesitate, afraid of upsetting people. But hesitation can be just as costly as making the wrong call. The best leaders own their decisions, take responsibility, and adjust when needed.

Group Decisions Are a Trap

Seeking input is valuable. But in the end, every decision needs a clear owner. Shared decisions create easy escape routes. When things go wrong, blame gets passed around, and no one is accountable. Worse, a single person can quietly sabotage a decision they didn't agree with.

Real leadership means stepping up and taking ownership. If others contribute to the choice, acknowledge their input—but own the final call.

Decisions Should Be Made By the Right People

Just because someone has authority doesn't mean they're the best person to decide. Proximity to the issue matters. The best organisations empower the people closest to the problem to make the call, rather than forcing decisions through layers of bureaucracy.

A senior leader's job isn't to make every decision—it's to ensure the right people are making the right calls. Leadership isn't about control; it's about enabling smart decision-making at every level.

Diversity of Thought Strengthens Decisions

A strong leader doesn't surround themselves with "yes" people. Different perspectives uncover risks, challenge assumptions, and surface better solutions. Encouraging debate prevents blind spots.

But once input has been gathered, decide. No endless loops of discussion. No waiting for universal agreement. Strong leaders know when to listen and when to move.

Bias and Assumptions Can Destroy Good Decisions

We all have blind spots. The way we frame problems, the sources we trust, and our past experiences shape our decisions. The best leaders question their thinking. They challenge their assumptions and seek out perspectives they might be missing.

The most dangerous leaders are those who believe they don't have biases.

If a Decision Isn't Communicated Clearly, It Doesn't Exist

A decision that isn't shared properly leads to confusion, resistance, and misalignment. It's not enough to make a choice—people need to understand it.

Explain not just what was decided, but why. Context creates buy-in. A leader who second-guesses, hedges, or lacks conviction creates doubt. Clarity builds confidence. If a decision is worth making, it's worth making sure everyone understands it.

Facts Don't Care About Feelings

Strong leaders deal with reality as it is, not as they wish it to be. Some decisions are hard. Some outcomes are painful. Agonising over facts won't change them.

When the facts are clear, don't overthink—make the call. Leadership isn't about always being right. It's about moving forward, adjusting when necessary, and having the courage to course correct.

Great Leaders Think Beyond the First Step

Every decision creates ripple effects. The best leaders anticipate second-order consequences. What happens after this choice? What happens next? And then what?

A decision that seems smart in the short term may create long-term problems. Short-sighted leadership fixes today's issue but causes tomorrow's failure. Strong leaders think beyond the immediate and make choices that hold up over time.

Balance Short-Term Needs with Long-Term Value

Leadership is a constant balancing act. There's always tension between what needs to be done now and what will pay off in the future.

The pressure for quick wins is real. But sacrificing long-term value for short-term results is a fast track to failure. Before making a call, ask:

- » Will this still make sense in a year?
- » Five years?
- » A decade?

The best leaders serve both the present and the future.

Track Your Decisions—Memory is Unreliable

No one remembers every detail. Without documentation, context is lost, mistakes are repeated, and progress is slowed.

Keeping a record of key decisions, along with why they were made, helps leaders refine their judgment. Patterns emerge. Trends become clear. A disciplined approach to tracking decisions turns experience into wisdom.

Filter Out the Noise

Not every issue deserves deep thought. Some problems are inflated by emotion, politics, or personal fears. Strong leaders strip away distractions and focus on what actually matters.

Before making a call, ask:
- » Am I acting out of fear?
- » Do I have a hidden agenda?
- » Is this really important, or just urgent?

Smart leaders separate signal from noise.

Listening First Leads to Better Decisions

Too many leaders rush to speak. They want to impose their perspective before understanding the full picture. But strong decisions come from deep understanding.

Great leaders listen first. They don't just hear the loudest voices. They seek out quiet insights, challenge assumptions, and create space for real discussion.

Encourage Debate—Dissent Strengthens Decisions

A team that always agrees is a team that isn't thinking critically. Disagreement isn't a threat—it's an asset. Debate surfaces risks, refines thinking, and strengthens choices.

Leaders who welcome challenge build better teams and better decisions. Leaders who fear dissent surround themselves with yes-men—and fail.

Integrity is Non-Negotiable

There will always be easier paths, more convenient choices, and shortcuts that offer quick wins. But trust is built on doing the right thing, even when it's hard.

People remember how decisions were made, not just what was decided. Leadership that compromises ethics for expedience loses credibility.

Decisiveness Requires Adaptability

Leadership isn't about sticking to a choice just to seem strong. The best leaders adapt when new information comes in. But changing course must be done for the right reasons—not out of fear or pressure.

Before reversing a decision, ask:

- » What new information justifies this change?
- » Will this lead to a better outcome?

Consistency matters, but rigidity is dangerous.

Some Decisions Are Final—Make Them Right

Not every decision can be undone. Some choices—hiring, strategy shifts, major investments—carry long-term consequences.

These require diligence, preparation, and deep thought. The worst mistakes happen when irreversible decisions are made carelessly.

Own Your Choices—Stand By Them

Weak leaders waver under pressure and backtrack at the first sign of discomfort. Strong leaders commit, follow through, and inspire confidence.

If you change course too easily, people stop trusting your decisions. Standing firm doesn't mean ignoring feedback—it means leading with conviction.

The Best Leaders Do the Right Thing, No Matter the Cost

The hardest decisions are often the right ones. They might be unpopular. They might be expensive. But doing the right thing builds credibility, trust, and lasting impact.

Leadership isn't about winning every argument or making the easiest choice. It's about standing for something greater.

The Best Leaders Make Hard Calls Before They Become Crises

If you're always making decisions under pressure, you're already behind. The best leaders don't wait for problems to explode—they see the warning signs, anticipate the risks, and act before things spiral. Avoiding tough calls doesn't make them go away—it just limits your options later. Leadership means tackling the hard decisions early, when you still have control, instead of waiting until there's no good choice left.

Overconfidence is Just as Dangerous as Indecision

Hesitation kills momentum, but rushing in blindly kills credibility. Decisiveness without wisdom is just arrogance. Some leaders mistake speed for strength, making reckless calls without questioning their own blind spots. Confidence should come from preparation and awareness, not ego. If you're making big decisions without challenging assumptions, stress-testing ideas, or listening to experience, you're not being bold—you're being reckless.

Side Quest
Water, Wheat, and the Weight of Decisions

The farm lay quiet in the midday sun, its fields a sea of golden wheat swaying gently in the breeze.

Arcanus led the team toward it, where a group of farmers stood gathered around a dishevelled middle-aged man holding a rusted plough.

The man—Lothar—had been speaking in a heated tone, but he fell silent as the strangers approached.

Arcanus raised a hand in greeting. "Good morrow, gentlemen. What seems to be the trouble here?"

Lothar sighed, clearly frustrated. "The irrigation channel broke last week. We're debating whether to patch it quickly or dig a new one entirely.

"The patch will get us through the season, but it won't last. Digging a new channel takes time we don't have if we want to harvest before the first frost."

Arcanus turned to Berik, the party's blacksmith-warrior, his second, and their middle manager of sorts.

"What do you think?"

Berik stroked his chin, thinking.

Then he stepped forward, his demeanour shifting—he had a plan.

"First, let's listen to everyone. What do the rest of you think?"

A young woman, her cheeks smudged with dirt, spoke first. "We should patch it. The crops need water now. If we wait, we'll lose a third of the harvest."

An older man shook his head. "Dig the new channel. We've patched it too many times already. If we don't fix it properly, it'll collapse again, and we'll lose even more next year."

Berik nodded thoughtfully, then turned back to Lothar.

"What's your real concern here? What's stopping you from deciding?"

Lothar hesitated, then said quietly, "If we dig the new channel, we'll need more hands than we have. It'll mean hiring workers from the next town, and I'm not sure we can afford it."

Berik crossed his arms, considering.

"I see. Let's weigh this out logically.

"A patch might save the crops this year, but you risk bigger losses next year.

"A new channel gives you long-term stability but stretches your resources now."

He paused, scanning the group.

"Let's reason this out.

"Everyone here, save us, has stakes. Your perspectives matter."

A spirited discussion followed, the farmers debating among themselves.

When the voices died down, Berik raised his hand for silence.

"I think we have enough information to go by.

"Your best option is to dig the new channel, and we'll help you organise the work.

"Arcanus, can you use magyck to speed up the digging?"

At this, Arcanus nodded.

Berik continued, "Sorche, you'll hire hands from the next town.

"We can pay them with part of this year's harvest if coin is tight—aye, Lothar?"

Lothar looked uneasy. "What if it's not enough?"

Berik held his gaze, firm.

"Then we'll take another look and adjust.

"If new information comes along, we'll re-evaluate.

"As it stands, this is your best option—short and long term.

"It's not about what's easy—it's about what lasts."

The farmers nodded reluctantly, and the party spent the afternoon helping to plan the construction of the new channel.

As they prepared to leave, Lothar approached Berik, holding out an old, dust-covered box.

"Thank you for your assistance, Smithy," he said. "This belonged to my father. He called it his Power Glove. Maybe it'll be useful to you."

Berik turned it over in his hands, chuckling at the ancient device.

"A relic of old times, huh?"

He strapped it to his belt, ready for the road ahead.

As the party left the farm, Arcanus glanced at Berik. "A fair decision, though not an easy one."

Berik shrugged. "The best decisions rarely are.

"But when you've got the facts, the values, and the vision, it's not about making everyone happy—it's about doing what's right."

> *"Every great decision creates ripples, like a huge boulder dropped in a lake. The ripples merge and rebound off the banks in unforeseeable ways. The heavier the decision, the larger the waves, the more uncertain the consequences."*
>
> — Doctor Who serial, Remembrance of the Daleks

Side Quest
Balancing the Scales

The party walked their horses across the cobbled streets, weaving through the bustling throng of merchants and villagers preparing for the annual Harvest Festival.

As they reached the town square, Sorche—the group's tactician—paused, her sharp gaze locking onto a heated argument between the town elder and a group of farmers.

"We can't divert the river!" one farmer shouted. "The fields will dry up!"

The elder shook his head. "If we don't, the festival grounds will flood, and we'll lose everything."

Sorche stepped forward, clearing her throat to announce her presence. "What's going on?"

The elder gestured toward the swollen river that ran alongside the town. "Unseasonal rains. If we don't reroute it, the festival's ruined. But the farmers claim they'll lose crops."

Sorche nodded, instantly understanding the danger.

Turning to the farmers, she asked, "How much of the fields would dry up?"

"Enough to cost us half the harvest," one replied. "And without that, no one eats through winter."

Sorche took a deep breath, weighing the consequences.

Flooding the festival grounds would impact morale, trade, and alliances.

But losing half the harvest threatened lives.

That was not an option.

"We can't allow that."

"But the festival—" the elder began.

"—will have to adapt," Sorche interrupted.

"Reroute the river, but not fully.

"Build temporary ditches to divert just enough water to keep the fields intact.

"The festival grounds will need reinforcement, and the celebration will be smaller—but it will take place.

"That solves both problems—a compromise."

The elder frowned. "The traders won't like that."

Sorche met his gaze, unwavering.

"Then tell them this: compromise protects the town.

"Without food, there's no trade, no alliances.

"Everyone sacrifices a little to ensure you all survive."

The elder nodded reluctantly before setting off to rally the villagers.

Sorche turned to the party, her expression resolute. "I think we can help them with the ditches.

"Quick decisions don't mean rash ones.

"The right call often costs something—but it's worth the price."

As they worked, one of the farmers muttered, "You don't shy away when you decide, do you?"

Sorche offered him a tough smile.

"The cost of regret outweighs the cost of standing firm.

"You make the call—and see it through."

Later, as the town rallied around the reinforced festival grounds, a villager approached Sorche, pressing a small pendant into her hand.

A lion-shaped emblem, roaring in defiance.

"A token of thanks, my lady," the villager said. "The last time someone stood for us, it was a king. He wore a crest like this."

Sorche turned it over, recognising the unmistakable emblem of Stormwind.

"The right choice isn't always the easiest," she murmured, tucking the pendant away.

With that, she rejoined the party—ready for whatever the journey might bring.

THE UNWRITTEN RULES

Decisions Aren't Just About Logic—Emotions Matter Too

In personal and professional settings, decisions are not always made purely based on logic and facts. People's emotions, beliefs, workplace politics, and relationships influence outcomes. Even if a logical choice seems obvious, others might resist due to personal stakes, other interests or feelings.

You Must Follow Up on Decisions, Not Just Announce Them

In leadership and teamwork, making a decision is only half the job. People don't always automatically follow through just because a choice was made. Communication, reminders, and follow-ups are needed to ensure execution.

People Expect Validation, Not Just Solutions

When someone shares a problem, they don't always want an immediate solution. Often, they just want to be heard and acknowledged. Jumping straight into problem-solving mode can make them feel unheard or dismissed.

Social Hierarchy Exists Including Among Equals

In social groups, friendships and interactions often have unspoken rules about who takes the lead, who organises events, or who is the most influential. Ignoring these dynamics can cause unintended conflicts.

THE MIRROR OF MASTERY

» What unintended consequences might my past decisions have had that I didn't anticipate at the time, and how could I train myself to think more in second-order effects in the future?

» How do I balance making decisions based on logic and facts while also accounting for the emotions, biases, and perspectives of others, even when they don't seem relevant to the best solution?

» When I struggle to communicate a decision or perspective effectively, what patterns emerge in how people misunderstand me, and how could I adjust my approach while staying true to my thinking style?

A GILDED EDGE

Biases – Get to know them

Confirmation Bias – Favouring information that supports your existing beliefs while ignoring contradictory evidence.

Anchoring Bias – Relying too heavily on the first piece of information received (the "anchor") when making decisions.

Availability Heuristic – Judging the likelihood of an event based on how easily examples come to mind.

Overconfidence Bias – Overestimating your own knowledge, abilities, or control over situations.

Sunk Cost Fallacy – Continuing an effort because of past investments, even when it no longer makes sense.

Halo Effect – Allowing one positive trait or impression of a person or thing to influence judgment in unrelated areas.

Recency Bias – Giving more weight to recent events and experiences than older ones.

Bandwagon Effect – Adopting beliefs or behaviours just because many others do.

Framing Effect – Being influenced by how information is presented (e.g., "90% survival rate" vs. "10% chance of death").

Status Quo Bias – Preferring things to remain the same, even when change would be beneficial.

Self-Serving Bias – Attributing successes to your own ability and failures to external factors.

Dunning-Kruger Effect – People with low ability overestimate their competence, while highly skilled people may underestimate theirs.

Hindsight Bias – Believing, after an event, that you "knew it all along" or that it was more predictable than it actually was.

Negativity Bias – Giving more attention and weight to negative experiences over positive ones.

Choice-Supportive Bias – Justifying past decisions by remembering them as better than they actually were.

CHAPTER 6

The Storm and the Calm

Main Quest
The Odyssey of Purposeful Leadership

Arcanus got the team an early start on the next stage of their journey. Their horses were well-rested, and, being the generous leader that he was, he sprung for a horse for Juju.

The elf graciously accepted, declaring that his poor shoes had seen better days.

Sore feet, however, had not stopped Juju from composing several more songs, and despite repeated warnings to keep a low profile, the bard seemed incapable of subtlety.

There was one last village between them and Darsura—one final night standing between them and the potential end of the world.

Naturally, they hadn't told Juju that.

Some information was on a 'need-to-know' basis.

And Juju didn't need to know.

Arcanus would come to regret that decision later.

Twelve long hours later

The sky had darkened, heavy with rain clouds, and as the group approached the forest's edge, the heavens finally opened.

A deluge of rain poured down, drenching them instantly.

While the fresh water was a relief, washing away the choking dust of a very, very long day, exhaustion had sapped their patience.

Tensions ran high.

Juju muttered curses under his breath, lamenting the ruin of his writing materials and his soaked lute.

Sorche, though miserable, held her tongue—barely.

Berik, on the other hand, looked ready to snap someone in two.

They dismounted, tending to their equally exhausted horses first.

Arcanus performed a safety and security spell over the camp and another to help the horses rest.

Once their tents were set up, they huddled around a weak campfire, drenched, drained, and thoroughly frustrated.

Twelve hours of travel had wrung them dry of both energy and humour.

The air was heavy and oppressive, thick with mosquitoes that wasted no time feasting on them.

After slapping at her arms and neck repeatedly, Sorche finally lost her patience.

"I'm so over this day.

"Nothing but choking dust for twelve hours, and now—bloody freakin' bugs!

"No, Berik, don't even show me that blasted map again, thinking you'll somehow offer a 'better campsite.'

"You know as well as I do that this forest stretches on for another couple of hours, and it does not get any better.

"This spot is as good as it's gonna get, and I'm done for the night.

"There is NO WAY I'm moving a single step further."

She turned to Arcanus, exasperated.

"Arcanus, can you spell these damn bugs away? They're bleeding me dry here!"

Berik, ever stubborn, simply shook his head, tapping the soggy map in his hands.

"This is a nightmare— we can't and shouldn't shelter beneath the trees during a storm like this!

"There's no windbreak, and for all we know, any manner of man or beast could be out there waiting to kill us.

"The last village is only a couple of hours away.

"We should push on— even if we're ALL DEAD TIRED!"

Juju, ever averse to conflict, had come to see these crazy people as his friends.

Desperate to ease the tension, he strummed a few chords on his waterlogged lute and began to sing an adjusted version of "Song of Rest."

The melody was mournful, heartfelt— and, for reasons unknown, it made Juju openly weep.

The sound of his crying only infuriated Berik further.

> *Under a starry sky, four friends doomed to fiiiiight!*
> *Caught in a storm, anger and scorn fills the airrrrr!*
> *The rift now formed, a sound of pain*
> *Is there a chaaance to chaaange?!*
> *The leader ris-HEY!*

Berik grabbed Juju's lute and smashed it against a tree, the wooden frame splintering on impact.

He showed no care for the bard, who now openly wept, mourning the loss of his beloved instrument, cradling its remains in his colourful patchwork cloak.

Arcanus frowned.

This wasn't like Berik.

The man was neither violent nor cruel— and this seemed wildly out of character.

"Berik, why did you do that?!"

His voice was sharp with genuine annoyance.

Berik's jaw tightened. "I couldn't stand his damned caterwauling anymore!"

His gaze burned as he turned on Arcanus.

"I warned you not to bring him along, but you didn't listen.

"This is what happens when you don't listen to members of your team, Arcanus."

Arcanus studied his friend carefully.

Berik was truly worked up, his temper fraying, just like Sorche's.

Something wasn't right.

Then—a shiver crawled up Arcanus's spine.

Magyck.

Dark magyck.

A rage enchantment.

That had to be it.

It hadn't affected him or Juju as badly as it had the others, but over the next few hours, unless he could reverse the spell, he too would fall victim to it.

And then, Juju would be left alone—surrounded by three demented, rage-filled souls.

Arcanus acted fast.

Grateful for the abundance of fresh rainwater, he began the counter-spell.

Muttering the incantation, he flicked water droplets toward his companions, who were still arguing at the top of their lungs.

> *Still waters and stormy skies,*
> *Let fury fade, and peace reside.*
> *Let the tempest cease and rest,*
> *Allow calm and joy to fill the breast.*

Arcanus repeated the spell for several minutes, his focus unwavering.

He could feel the shift when the enchantment began to dissipate—

The air lightened, the oppressive weight lifting as they breathed easier.

"Everyone alright?"

His companions still wore somewhat disgruntled expressions, but the fury had faded.

Not entirely—but enough.

It would take time before they were truly themselves again.

A familiar voice echoed in Arcanus's mind—the High Elder, speaking to him during a previous assignment when he had faced a similar challenge.

"Make sure you get a handle on any conflict areas within your team.

"It's up to you to face it head-on, Arcanus.

"Some people need to be told in plain words what the objectives of the mission are—make sure they understand.

"I can tell you this: in all my years as High Elder, most conflict situations stem from misunderstandings—people either misunderstand each other, or they misunderstand what's required of them.

"It's your job to be clear, to think constructively.

"Try and keep emotion out of it—look at the situation from a different perspective before you set forth a solution."

The memory lingered, and with it, another piece of advice:

Never go to sleep angry.

Though, Arcanus wasn't sure the High Elder had been referring to supernatural rage when he said that.

Still, the sentiment remained.

"Everyone, let's get some sleep.
"Tomorrow will be a better day. I'll take first watch."
"Juju—keep singing. It soothes me."

With a few groans, muttered curses, and exhausted sighs, the group rolled out their sleeping bags.

Before long, camp had settled into silence—

Save for Juju's quiet, melancholic song.

Berik would take the next watch, and Sorche would take the final shift before dawn.

Tomorrow was going to be another long day.

Arcanus could only hope it would be less eventful.

"Peacemakers are people who breathe grace."

"Everyone encounters conflict—whether it be with a coworker, family member, friend, or complete stranger."

— Ken Sande & Kevin Johnson, Resolving Everyday Conflict

"Teams that have little or no conflict are rarely high performing."

"Your leadership career will be so much happier and so much more fulfilling if you learn to handle conflict confidently and comfortably."

"Managing the conflict so that it remains constructive and focused on shared excellence rather than individual point scoring can be really difficult."

— Martin G. Moore, No Bullsh!t Leadership

Several hours later

After a quick but hearty breakfast, the party saddled up and set out once more.

Arcanus had taken precautionary measures, warding each member against supernatural curses and ailments, ensuring they wouldn't be affected again.

Juju, being Elf-kind, was naturally less susceptible to magyckal foul play—but he was not immune.

There were still ways for him to be affected.

As it was, Berik and Sorche were still shaking off the remnants of the rage enchantment.

Arcanus could only hope that by the time they reached the last village, both of them would have returned to normal.

Slight bickering aside, the group remained mostly quiet, each keeping their thoughts to themselves.

Juju, however, occasionally hummed a light tune under his breath, scribbling in what appeared to be a well-worn journal.

Several hours later – outskirts of the last village before Darsura

Several hours later, the party finally arrived at the village of Fir Bolge.

Arcanus checked them into the local inn while Berik led the horses to the stables, carefully instructing the stable lad on the proper way to care for them.

Their horses were valuable, and they always made it a point to ensure their well-being.

Juju, meanwhile, announced he was heading to the local pub.

Sorche, raising a sceptical brow, decided to go with him.

A good decision.

Someone needed to keep an eye on Juju.

What neither of them knew was that Berik had seen Juju heading toward the pub.

Now that the effects of the rage enchantment had finally worn off, Berik was back to his usual, watchful self.

He noticed Sorche hurrying after Juju and exhaled in relief—but he also wondered whether Sorche could truly handle Juju and his 'extraness.'

Probably not.

At the Pub

Sorche and Juju entered the lively tavern together.

She immediately claimed a corner table, ordering two light ales.

She had no intention of dealing with a drunken Juju tonight.

Juju, however, had other plans.

The moment he spotted a small stage, he hopped onto it, cleared his throat, and belted out a bawdy tune.

The locals roared with laughter, thoroughly entertained.

Relieved that his antics had nothing to do with them, Sorche turned her attention to the innkeeper, hoping to gather some useful information.

She began questioning him about the comings and goings of strangers in the village.

She didn't notice Berik slip into the pub.

Juju, completely engrossed in his next song, missed Berik's entrance as well.

And, believing the ill-mannered blacksmith to be elsewhere, the bard decided to sing a familiar tune.

One version of the Song of Rest—

A song that Berik and Sorche had come to know all too well.

> *Draw near, brave travellers ye,*
> *And listen to a story of heroes (so I've been told...).*
> *A trio strange with quirks and more,*

Who've brought mayhem to every door...
Berik's face darkens dramatically.
First is the warrior, big and sulky,
Face like thunder, always brooding.
Swings his sword-OOOF

Juju was dragged off stage by a furious Berik, who muttered apologies to the patrons on behalf of 'his drunk friend.'

The bard protested loudly, but Berik wasn't listening.

Someone might have overheard.

He hauled Juju outside, shoving him against the pub's stone wall.

"You reckless fool!" Berik snarled, his eyes burning with fury.

Sorche rushed after them, stepping between the two men. "Berik, enough!"

But Berik was like a bull seeing red.

He was too enraged to listen, too furious to forgive such a sloppy mistake.

He pointed a finger at Sorche, his voice sharp.

"Handle Juju—before he gets us all killed."

Then, without another word, he stormed off down the road, disappearing into the shadows of the village.

> *"Whenever smart and well-intentioned people avoid confronting obstacles, they disempower employees and undermine change."*
>
> *"Effective leaders help others to understand the necessity of change and to accept a common vision of the desired outcome."*

> "Without credible communication, and a lot of it, the hearts and minds of others are never captured."
>
> — John P. Kotter, Change

> "Winners quit all the time. They just quit the right stuff at the right time."
>
> "If you cannot make it through the Dip, do not start."
>
> — Seth Godin, The Dip

An hour later

Juju and Sorche were laughing at Arcanus's joke just as Berik strolled in.

Arcanus was glad his friend had made it in time for dinner—

A hungry Berik was a grouchy Berik.

Curiously, Berik seemed to be in a good mood, though his gaze darkened the moment it landed on Juju.

If Berik had his way, he would probably lock the bard in a room just to keep him from causing trouble.

But Juju was a grown Elf, not a child.

And Arcanus, for one, was tired of all the bitching and infighting between the two of them.

It was time to set them straight.

But first—

A bath.

A long soak in what might be his last bath for a very long time.

After that, he planned to eat dinner in his room, in peace, before tackling these two stubborn fools.

The Next Morning

Arcanus's bath had been so relaxing, he fell asleep in the tub, completely forgoing dinner and his plan to put Berik and Juju back in their place.

By the time he awoke the next morning, the two had somehow gotten over their conflict.

That didn't mean he was letting it slide.

After everyone finished breakfast, they headed for the stables.

Once there, Arcanus cleared his throat, fixing Berik and Juju with a pointed stare until they stopped what they were doing and looked at him.

"You do understand that your behaviour was completely unacceptable, right?"

His voice was calm but firm.

"You are in this, working together, for a small period of time—remember that.

"Do I want to let one of you go? No.

"We work well as a team, and our newest addition has his own place within this circle.

"We are placed under pressure, in life-or-death situations, constantly. That means we need to learn about conflict— and how to handle it.

"It does not do to fall to pieces or fly into a rage if we don't get our way.

"We are in this together. If one of us fails, we all fail."

He let that sink in for a moment, his gaze unwavering.

"If you're seeking individual glory and fame, this quest is not for you.

"I need people who are invested in the mission, in us— just as I am invested in all of you."

Arcanus took a deep breath.

There was no point sugarcoating it now.

"I'm not going to lie to you at this point—there's a good chance we may die from here on out."

Juju's eyes widened slightly.

"I'm sorry I left that out at the start, Juju, but there it is. We may die.

"I would hope that each of you cares enough about each other, yourself, and this mission to put your grievances aside and put your best foot forward from here on out.

"If you cannot give me that, you are free to leave."

He let his words linger in the air.

"Take a few minutes and think it through.

"I hope to see you all at the mountain pass."

With a heavy heart, Arcanus mounted his horse and rode ahead.

He hoped they were mature enough to trust one another, to see this through.

To set aside their conflict and focus on the bigger picture.

Because, after all—

The fate of the world depended on this ragtag bunch making it to the end.

EDICTS OF THE WISE

Mastering Conflict: Step In, Don't Step Back

Conflict is a paradox. We avoid it, yet the only way to handle it well is to face it head-on. Avoiding conflict makes it worse. Engaging with it builds confidence and skill. People are both incredible and difficult, and conflict will expose you to the full range of emotions. You won't always get it right—but that's not the goal. What matters is showing up, engaging, and learning as you go.

Conflict Avoidance is Just Delayed Damage

Ignoring conflict doesn't make it go away—it just lets it grow in the dark. Unspoken frustrations don't fade over time; they build pressure until they explode. Leaders who dodge tough conversations aren't keeping the peace—they're setting the stage for a bigger mess later. If something needs addressing, deal with it now. Letting it fester only makes the fallout worse.

Embrace Discomfort—It's a Sign of Growth

Leaning into conflict won't feel natural at first. It will stretch you. It will test you. You'll feel the urge to back off, but that discomfort means you're growing. The more you do it, the more natural it becomes. Instead of dreading conflict, you'll start to see it as an opportunity—to clear the air, strengthen relationships, and solve real problems.

Most conflicts don't come from bad intentions. They come from misunderstandings. Clarity is your best defence. Set expectations early. If something is unclear, ask. If expectations are misaligned, fix them. Unspoken rules are landmines—expose them and replace them with open dialogue.

Address Issues Early—Don't Let Them Fester

Small annoyances grow into major problems when left unchecked. The sooner you engage, the easier the resolution. There's wisdom in the old saying: don't let the sun go down on an issue. Problems don't disappear on their own—they escalate.

When navigating conflict, keep the mission in focus. Are you all working toward the same goal? If not, that's the real issue. Align first, solve second. Grounding the discussion in shared objectives makes it less personal and more productive.

Emotional Intelligence Separates Conflict from Resolution

Every conflict has two layers—the issue itself and the emotions behind it. If you only focus on the surface-level disagreement and ignore what's fuelling it, you'll never get a real resolution. Frustration, insecurity, fear, or ego often amplify conflict more than the actual problem or misunderstanding. Strong leaders don't just react to the argument—they read the emotions, manage them first, and then solve the real issue.

Listen First—Then Solve

Jumping into solution mode too fast is a mistake. Seek to understand before you try to fix. Take a breath. Listen. Ask thoughtful questions. Let people explain their side fully. A rushed response can miss the real issue.

Adopt a win-win mindset. Some perspectives may seem too far apart to reconcile. That's normal. The goal isn't to "win" the argument—it's to find a path forward that works for everyone. The best resolutions respect all parties while keeping the bigger picture in mind.

Feedback Is an Opportunity, Not an Attack

Great leaders use conflict to help people grow. Recognise strengths in others and connect them to solutions. Feedback should build people up, not tear them down. A well-handled disagreement can strengthen a team instead of dividing it.

Respect matters more than popularity. People don't have to like you, but they do need to respect you. Integrity and consistency earn trust, even when your decisions aren't popular. Set boundaries. Maintain professionalism. Handle conflict with maturity.

Be Friendly, But Not Friends

There's a difference between having good relationships with your team and becoming too close. Blurring personal and professional lines complicates decision-making. Friendships at work can create bias, cloud judgment, and make leadership harder than it needs to be.

Own the Hard Calls—Lead with Courage

The right path isn't always the easy one. Leadership often means making hard decisions that won't make everyone happy. That's the job. The goal is not to be liked—it's to lead well.

Have your people's backs. Say it again—have your people's backs. Responsibility stops with you. Never throw your team under the bus. If something goes wrong, own it. Accountability starts at the top.

Give Feedback That Actually Works

Forget the "criticism sandwich"—it doesn't work. Instead, be direct, practical, and tie feedback to measurable results. People can't improve if they don't know what to fix. Focus on actions, not personalities. Be specific, and make sure feedback leads to growth.

Create a culture where feedback is frequent and expected. Teams that give and receive feedback regularly improve faster. If people hesitate to speak up, something is wrong. Make honesty the norm, not an exception.

One-on-one feedback should be private. Group feedback should involve everyone. No secret meetings. No hidden agendas. Transparency builds trust.

Keep Records—Documentation Prevents Drama

Take notes. Ask questions. Document key conversations. When emotions run high, facts matter. Clear records keep you objective and prevent misunderstandings.

If it's not written down, it didn't happen. Keeping track of past discussions helps spot patterns, track progress, and ensure accountability.

Find the Right Role for the Right Person

Not everyone is in the right seat on the bus. Some people are in the wrong role. If someone isn't thriving, help them find a better fit. And if there isn't a place for them in the team, be willing to make the tough call and let them go.

Handling these transitions with fairness and respect is key. The wrong person in the wrong role slows down the team. Great leadership means making sure everyone is set up to succeed.

Stay Objective—Emotions Cloud Judgment

Conflict resolution isn't about emotion—it's about clarity. Approach discussions with a clear head and grounded questions. Emotional reactions can make things worse. Stay focused on facts and solutions.

Power struggles have no place in conflict resolution. Dominating the conversation only creates resistance. The goal isn't to "win" the argument—it's to find a way forward.

Understand the "Why" Behind Someone's Position

Dig deeper. Why does someone feel strongly about an issue? What are they actually fighting for? People rarely argue just to argue. There's always a deeper reason—find it. Understanding their motivations helps you find solutions that address their real concerns.

Peace-making Isn't Weakness

Being a peacemaker doesn't mean giving in. It means finding fair, balanced outcomes. Avoid the extremes—don't attack, don't retreat. Stand firm in finding a resolution that benefits everyone.

Transparency and integrity are non-negotiable. People respect leaders who operate above reproach. But transparency doesn't mean sharing everything—some details don't need to be public. Knowing what to share and what to keep private is a leadership skill.

Not Every Conflict Needs to Be Resolved

Sometimes, walking away is the right choice. Not every disagreement will lead to resolution. If the effort to fix it outweighs the benefit, it may be time to move on.

The best leaders know when to push for a resolution and when to let go. If a conflict isn't productive or is draining too much energy, redirect that focus elsewhere.

If You Don't Know What's Right, You Can't Fight for It

Before stepping into issue or concern, be certain about what actually matters. Principles, not emotions, should guide your stance. If you're unclear on what's right, you're just arguing to win, not to lead.

How do you find what's right? Step back and ask: What are the facts, not just the feelings? What are the core values at play? What outcome serves the mission, not just individual preferences? Seek multiple perspectives, challenge your own assumptions, and be willing to adjust if new information changes the picture. Seek truth before you seek resolution—otherwise, you're just adding noise to the fight.

Lead with Strength, Fairness, and Confidence

Conflict is unavoidable. How you handle it defines you as a leader. The best leaders don't dodge tough conversations—they step into them with clarity, purpose, and respect.

- » Address issues early—don't wait for them to explode.
- » Listen first, then solve.
- » Own the hard calls, even when they're unpopular.
- » Keep feedback direct, fair, and tied to growth.
- » Set boundaries—be friendly, but not friends.
- » Document everything—facts beat emotions.
- » Find the right people for the right roles.
- » Stay objective—power struggles don't solve problems.
- » Understand what's really driving someone's stance.
- » Know when to walk away.

Handling conflict well isn't about winning—it's about building stronger teams, clearer expectations, and better outcomes. Master it, and you'll not only become a better leader—you'll build a team that trusts, respects, and follows you.

Side Quest
Trust, Trials, and the Path Forward

Berik looked around, surprised.

Somehow, he'd ended up on a forest trail, and from the look of it, he'd gone at least a mile into the woods.

The dense trees loomed around him, their presence creating a sense of enclosure—almost like being hugged.

As he walked, he felt his mood lighten, the tension from earlier easing with each step.

Then—a branch snapped.

Berik instantly stopped, scanning his surroundings.

A bend in the path lay ahead.

The faint creak of wood and low grunts caught his attention.

He jogged forward, rounding the bend to find a young man struggling.

His cart was hopelessly stuck in the mud.

The mule attached to it—clearly exhausted—stood trembling, her thin legs barely able to hold her weight.

Berik felt a pang of sympathy for the poor creature, struggling against an immovable force—

At least, the way the man was going about it.

Stepping forward, Berik rested his axes across his shoulders.

"Looks like you've got trouble, friend."

His tone was even, measured.

The young man patted the mule's ears, then suddenly burst into tears, streaks of mud and exhaustion lining his face.

"My father is going to kill me!"

"These goods were meant for an outpost nearby, but we've been stuck for half an hour!

"And Shelly— she's exhausted.

"I shouldn't have used this shortcut. I had a bad feeling, but I ignored it to save time!"

Berik clapped the fellow across the shoulders, then crossed his arms, surveying the scene.

"Shortcut, huh?

"Sometimes the easy path isn't the right one.

"Why didn't you go for help?"

The young man sniffled, shrugged, then stuck out his hand in greeting.

"Johan.

"I guess I thought I could handle it…"

Berik shook the offered hand.

"I can see Shelly's been struggling.

"She's as tired as you look.

"Unhitch her and take her over to the grass.

"She needs a good rest, and tonight, make sure you groom her well and give her extra feed."

Johan sniffled again, nodding, then waved toward the road.

Berik turned, watching as several figures approached.

"Your people?"

Johan nodded, introducing them.

Berik crouched, picking up a broken strap from the cart.

"Clearly, hauling heavy loads isn't exactly your forte.

"Let's figure this out."

He turned to the newcomers, issuing clear instructions.

"Rina, get Shelly some water and her feed bag.

"Trog, help me lighten this load.

"Sira, make sure these crates are secured for carrying on foot.

Then, he pointed at Johan.

"And you—what's your best skill?"

The man hesitated, then muttered,

"I'm good with maps.

"I can find paths hidden from the common gaze."

At Berik's raised brow, Johan blushed.

"I'm usually good with maps.

"The extra rainfall must have altered the path, creating this muddy pit."

Berik nodded, satisfied.

"You'll guide us to the outpost while we carry the supplies.

"Leave the hauling to those better suited for it."

As the group redistributed the load, Berik pulled Johan aside for a quiet word.

"You need to be honest about your limits.

"Trying to do things you're not equipped for doesn't just hurt you—

"It hurts the people counting on you.

"And wonderful creatures like Shelly.

"Next time, think before you leap— or take on more than you can handle."

Johan's shoulders relaxed.

"I will. Thanks for helping us figure this out."

Berik nodded. "Your friends were with you on this trip.

"That means having each other's backs.

"Calling them out when they're on the wrong path—

"And helping them find the right one.

"You do that for them— and they'll return the favour."

Hours Later

As the group finally reached the outpost, their supplies intact, Johan grinned.

"You've got a way of seeing things clearly, even when it seems hopeless.

"Like... like that relic hunter I heard about.

"You ever come across him on your travels?"

Berik raised an eyebrow.

"The one with the hat and whip?"

He smirked. "Let's just say I've dodged my share of rolling boulders, too."

Laughter rippled through the group as they set down the last crate.

A valuable lesson had been learned by all—

Find where people shine, and the whole team grows stronger.

Berik's dual axes rested lightly at his sides, ready for whatever came next.

> *"Sometimes, the only way to win is not to play."*
> — 1983 film, Wargames

The forest trail was unusually quiet, the dense canopy above filtering dappled sunlight onto the earthy ground.

Arcanus rode in thoughtful silence, lost in his own reflections, when the sound of galloping hooves reached his ears.

He glanced over his shoulder—

The team had caught up.

Not only that—everyone was here.

A warmth spread through his chest.

They had resolved their conflict.

They had achieved the best outcome possible.

Arcanus nodded to each of them, and one by one, they nodded back.

Berik cleared his throat.

"Arcanus, we all had a long chat and have come to terms with each other's presence on this mission."

His voice was calm, measured—genuine.

"In my life, trust is earned, not given.

"And you have certainly earned mine over all the years we've known each other.

"You have my trust, and I stand by your decision.

"I may quibble here and there, but seeing the bigger picture, I agree—

"They are good additions to the team."

Berik turned to Sorche and Juju.

"For my part— I apologise for not offering a warmer welcome at first.

"It was never personal.

"Arcanus is right—we do need you.

"And you are valued."

Sorche and Juju exchanged glances before offering Berik small smiles, grateful that they were no longer the object of his wrath.

Juju, ever the bard, began to hum a tune.

A moment later, Arcanus started whistling along.

Berik sighed but smirked.

It was going to be a fine day.

Arcanus could feel it.

Side Quest
The Shop Between the Trees

Arcanus led the group forward, his steps steady, until he noticed a faint glow emanating from his staff.

How odd.

He furrowed his brow, but before he could dwell on it, the party came upon a peculiar sight.

Nestled between the towering trees stood a small, ramshackle store.

Its bronze sign swayed gently in the breeze; the words etched in elegant script:

"Snickett's Curiosities – Rare Items for the Discerning Traveler."

Sorche narrowed her eyes, taking in the twisted metal chimneys and mismatched windows.

"Odd place for a shop," she muttered.

"No town for miles, and this store just happens to be here..."

Berik grunted, his fingers twitching toward an axe.

"Be careful and keep your eyes open."

Arcanus dismounted, motioning for Sorche to follow.

"Perhaps that's the point," he mused.

Inside the Shop

The creaky door swung open, revealing a dimly lit space.

Shelves overflowed with strange artifacts, dusty tomes, and vials filled with swirling liquids.

Arcanus's senses told him that half of it was for show.

The other half?

That was the real question.

At the counter stood a tall, thin elf, his sharp smile gleaming.

His robes shimmered like starlight.

Arcanus would have killed for one like it—

And at that moment, his rash flared up again.

Drat this rash.

The elf tilted his head, his voice smooth as silk.

"Ah, customers."

"Welcome! I'm Snickett.

"What brings you to my little store?"
Arcanus stepped forward.
"We seek a Lumina Shard."
His voice was even, controlled.
"It is said to stabilise magyck in unstable lands."
Snickett's smile tightened.
His hands rubbed together, calculating.
"Ah, a rare treasure, indeed.
"But such things do not come cheaply."
The air grew tense.
Arcanus and Sorche exchanged wary glances.
They knew exactly what kind of merchant they were dealing with.
Thankfully, Arcanus had laid a powerful yet undetectable charm on his staff—
To Snickett's eyes, it appeared nothing more than an old, ratty limb.
Still, the elf's sharp, hungry gaze flickered across them, his words edged with manipulation.
Arcanus leaned against his staff, his tone calm.
"What would you like in exchange?"
Snickett hesitated—surprised.
Then, choosing his words carefully, he spoke.
"My wares are priceless… but they cannot help me repair the protective wards on this shop.
"Without them, I'll soon be overrun by the creatures of the forest."
Arcanus slowly nodded.
"You offer rare items, but your protection falters.
"A conundrum, wouldn't you say?"
Snickett smirked.
"Indeed…"

Arcanus continued, his voice steady.

"You need security to ensure the safety of your wares.

"We will repair your wards, and in return, we will take the shard as payment.

"A balanced exchange. What do you say?"

Snickett tilted his head, intrigued.

His demeanour softened.

"Fair.

"Unusual for a human.

"You trust me not to demand more?"

Arcanus held his gaze.

"We trust ourselves to hold true.

"We seek peace, not advantage.

"You'll find no power games here."

A long pause.

Then—

A genuine smile.

"A rare kind of negotiation, indeed."

Snickett nodded.

"Very well. The shard is yours once the wards are complete.

"You have my word."

A Deal Sealed in Balance

Arcanus worked in silence, restoring the intricate magyck that shielded the shop.

As he finished, Snickett handed over the Lumina Shard.

But before they left, the elf spoke again, his voice thoughtful.

"Few would have the stones to negotiate with such balance and clarity.

"You remind me of an old saying: 'Courage is not the absence of fear, but the mastery of it.'"

Arcanus nodded knowingly.

"Wise words, old one.

"Passed down, perhaps, by someone holding a wand shaped like a phoenix feather?"

Snickett blinked.

For the briefest moment, recognition flickered across his face.

But he said nothing more.

As They Departed

Sorche glanced back.

"Why didn't you just push him to hand it over?"

"He needed you more than you needed him."

Arcanus smiled faintly.

"Force creates enemies, not peace.

"A fair deal serves everyone—until it doesn't.

"That's when you walk away."

His eyes twinkled with amused light.

"And besides—

"A Lumina Shard freely given shines brighter."

THE UNWRITTEN RULES

Directness is a Tool—Use It Wisely

Being direct is efficient, but social interactions aren't always about efficiency. Cutting people off, being overly blunt, or shutting down ideas too fast can make you seem dismissive—even if you might be right. There's a rhythm to the conversation and jumping in too hard disrupts it. Pausing before responding and softening your approach doesn't mean being vague—it means making sure your message actually lands. Instead of "That won't work," try "I see your point, but here's what I'm thinking..." It has the same message and a better impact.

People Don't Always Say Exactly What They Mean—Pay Attention

Not everything is spelled out. Hesitation, tone, and phrasing can tell you more than the words themselves. When someone says, "I guess that could work..." there is likely doubt in their voice, so they probably don't mean yes. Instead of assuming, clarify. Ask, "Would you prefer a different option?" or "What's your take on it?" Reading between the lines is a skill—leaders who master it make better decisions and avoid unnecessary conflict.

Hierarchy Exists, Even When It's Casual

Even in laid-back workplaces where people call the boss by their first name, unspoken rules still apply. Leadership structures exist, and decisions carry different weight depending on who makes them. Ignoring hierarchy doesn't make it disappear—it just makes you oblivious to how things actually work. If you want to navigate leadership effectively, understand the balance between informality and respect (Keep your noticing tuned in).

Silence Can Mean Many Things—Learn to Read It

Not all silence is agreement. Sometimes it's thoughtful reflection, quiet resistance, discomfort, or just a lack of engagement. Assuming silence means approval is a mistake. If you're leading a discussion and people aren't responding, don't just move on—pause, check in, and invite input. A simple "Does that align with what you're thinking?" or "I'd love to hear your take" can reveal what's really going on. Good leaders listen to what's said. Great leaders notice what isn't.

THE MIRROR OF MASTERY

» How can I tell when a conflict is about logic and facts versus emotions and relationships?

» How do I recognise when persistence is helping me push through challenges versus when quitting is the right choice?

» How do I determine when to adapt my approach versus when to stand firm on my principles?

CHAPTER 7

The Ledger and the Blueprint

Main Quest

The Odyssey of Purposeful Leadership

Arcanus knew he was the one holding everyone accountable.

Now that Sorche had accepted responsibility for keeping an eye on Juju—well, Juju's loose tongue—things would flow more smoothly.

It was easy to shove responsibility onto another to avoid blame.

Still—

The High Elder had trained him as a leader.

He saw that now.

All the assessments and tests…

All the challenges…

Everything had led up to this moment.

He had curated this team, corrected their behaviours when needed, delegated when necessary, and stepped up to hold them accountable.

He had matured.

If only the High Elder could see him now…

Arcanus was not one for accolades, but he did want the old man to know—

All those years studying under him had proved infinitely valuable.

A Harsh and Unforgiving Path

The cold wind shrieked around the jagged mountain peaks, carrying with it whispers of danger and destiny.

Arcanus tightened his cloak, feeling the sting of the elements.

His staff pulsed faintly with light, responding to the danger ahead.

Even the rash—his ever-persistent, irritating rash—

Had gone quiet.

As if it, too, knew they were walking a narrow path.

How ironic.

Behind him, his companions followed closely:

Berik, the stalwart warrior, clad in gleaming plate armour, axes resting at his sides.

Sorche, the enigmatic strategist, her sharp green eyes scanning the shadows.

Juju, the elven bard, humming cheerfully despite the harsh environment, his cloak wrapped snugly around his slender frame.

Yes.

He had chosen well.

The Last Stretch

Arcanus exhaled, bracing himself.

"Darsura lies just beyond this ridge," he said, voice steady despite the tension gripping his heart.

"Rafe's stronghold awaits us."

Berik grunted, adjusting his grip on his axes.

"'Bout time.

"All this sneaking around doesn't sit well with me.

"Let's breach those walls and get it over with."

He glanced at Arcanus.

"I have contacts within the army units.

"They've promised to help us gain entry."

Sorche shot him a sharp look.

"Charging in without a plan is a good way to get us killed.

"Arcanus has led us well so far; let's trust his judgment."

Juju's voice broke the tension.

"Let us not forget, my friends, the importance of harmony in our endeavour.

"Discord will not serve us against a foe like this dark wizard."

He paused, glancing at Arcanus.

"By the way, thank you for letting me into your inner circle."

Arcanus smirked.

"It's not my inner circle, Juju.

"It was a group decision that you be informed.

"So you would be forewarned—and therefore, forearmed."

Juju waved a dismissive hand.

"Yes, yes, but truly—thank you."

Arcanus chuckled.

Juju always had a way of diffusing conflict and creating humour.

The bard's music had been a source of strength throughout the latter half of their journey—

Despite Berik thinking him a huge pain in the ass.

Despite Berik smashing his lute—

(which he had promised to replace).

Even Berik had begrudgingly admitted the songs were soothing.

Juju was a magyckal being, and his songs were infused with warmth and clarity.

It was truly difficult to stay in a foul mood around him for long.

Darsura, at Last

As the party crested the ridge, the stronghold of Darsura came into view.

A fortress of shadows and steel, its blackened spires rose defiantly against the storm-darkened sky.

Torches burned along the walls, casting eerie flickers of light against massive iron gates.

A stronghold built for war.

For power.

For dominion.

Arcanus narrowed his eyes.

They had arrived.

Several hours later

The stronghold of Darsura appeared as if it had been carved into the very mountain itself, a dark monolith clinging to the rock face like a fortress born of the earth's own fury.

Arcanus knew its history well.

This was no mere fortress—

It was a triumph of war, an impregnable bastion crafted by master builders who had poured their skill, blood, and genius into its walls.

Now, standing before it, he understood why.

Built straight into the mountainside, its blackened spires stretched toward the heavens, almost as if they were pulling the sky itself down.

The exterior bristled with massive copper gears and intricate steam-powered machinery, their rhythmic churning sending great plumes of smoke into the frigid air.

Pipes of all sizes snaked along the fortress walls, pulsating with an eerie blue light—

A marriage of magyck and machinery.

Above them, enormous turbines spun, their mechanical hum a constant, thrumming heartbeat of power.

Their energy fuelled the stronghold's defences—

And maintained the unnatural storms that perpetually swirled around its peaks.

The party stood in silence, absorbing the terrifying beauty of the stronghold.

Arcanus exhaled sharply.

"The magyckal defences will be daunting," he said.

"But we have the advantage of surprise. Here's the plan."

His gaze swept over his team.

"Sorche—scout ahead. Get us a way inside.

"Berik—stay close and be ready for combat.

"Juju—have your songs and lute at the ready.

"We'll need your magyck to bolster our strength."

A deep red blush spread across Juju's cheeks.

He mumbled something.

Arcanus narrowed his eyes.

"Juju, what's the problem?"

The bard shifted uneasily.

"I… didn't repair my lute yet."

Arcanus stared at him.

"What?"

Juju winced.

"I was going to. I planned to. But it… slipped my mind and—"

Arcanus threw up a hand.

"What do you mean it slipped your mind?

"I told you we needed your help, Juju.

"You had a clear objective. Why didn't you say something earlier?!"

Juju winced again.

"By the time I remembered, it was too late. We had already left the last village.

"And, well... I was afraid to say something then."

Arcanus rubbed his temple, feeling the frustration boil.

This oversight could endanger the mission.

Juju's lute was a magyckal instrument.

And repair spells were unpredictable.

If the instrument rejected the spell...

They would be down a powerful support.

And Arcanus was unsure whether Juju's voice alone could bolster their strength the way the lute's magyck-infused melodies could.

Arcanus sighed heavily.

"Juju, you should have told me the moment you remembered.

"Each of us is accountable for the skills we bring into battle.

"If we can't be upfront about our limitations, we're in trouble."

Juju nodded miserably, his fingers clutching the broken pieces of his lute.

"I will need your help with the repair spell," Arcanus said at last.

"These things can backfire. Your influence will help the lute accept the restoration."

Juju perked up slightly, eager to redeem himself.

He nodded.

A Delicate Repair

Arcanus began chanting, weaving the threads of restoration magyck.

Juju joined him, his melodious voice intertwining with the spell, the notes laced with healing power.

The wooden fragments of the lute shuddered—

Then began to knit together.

Strands of golden light wrapped around it, fusing the pieces until—

It was whole once more.

Juju held it reverently, running his fingers along the smooth wood, awe-struck.

"It worked…"

Arcanus exhaled, relieved.

"Good. Try not to break it again."

Juju nodded quickly, cradling the lute like a sacred relic.

Final Preparations

Arcanus turned back to the group.

"Now—before the distraction.

"I have brought all the help I need, save for the Skrol.

"Once we breach the sanctum of the Wizard, I will call to it."

His gaze sharpened.

"We've discussed our plans, adjusted them, then readjusted them.

"But remember—nothing is foolproof.

"Be careful. Stay sharp."

The team nodded, their expressions resolute.

They had placed their faith and trust in him.

Sorche disappeared into the darkness, her movements silent as the grave.

The rest of them carefully descended.

Each step brought them closer—

To Rafe.

To the Skrol.

To the heart of darkness itself.

> *"To achieve goals you've never achieved before, you need to start doing things you've never done before."*
>
> *"Accountability breeds response-ability."*
>
> *"Begin with the end in mind."*
>
> *"Make time for planning: Wars are won in the general's tent."*
>
> *"The key is not to prioritise what's on your schedule, but to schedule your priorities."*
>
> — Stephen R. Covey, The 7 Habits of Highly Effective People

Two hours later, they stood before a concealed entrance that Sorche had discovered. The dense shadows of the fortress loomed overhead, swallowing the dim light of the overcast sky. Sorche emerged from the darkness, her face grim.

"The guards are few, but they're not... ordinary," she said, voice hushed. "Rafe's magyck has changed them. They're deformed, no longer human. I don't know how to explain it."

Berik gripped his axes tightly.

"We'll cut them down and show no quarter to those serving a monster!"

Sorche snorted, shaking her head.

"Berik, listen to me. These beasts are neither human nor animal; they do not appear to think at all. I watched them for an hour. They kill everything that moves—one nearly killed another guard!"

Berik said nothing.

This was not good news.

Arcanus took a deep breath. "Let's go."

His staff flared brighter as he whispered a protection and

concealment spell over the group. They slipped into the fortress, the air within thick with an unnatural chill.

The corridors were lined with jagged runes, almost appearing to twist and writhe under their gaze, faint whispers of the dead echoing through the stone.

First Blood

The first fight came all too soon.

Grotesque, mutated guards lunged from the shadows, their forms twisted beyond recognition.

Berik met them head-on, his dual axes cleaving through their ranks with brutal efficiency.

Sorche moved like a phantom, weaving between their strikes, her daggers finding soft, vulnerable flesh with deadly precision.

It was both hideous and mesmerising to watch.

Juju's voice lilted through the chaos, his song weaving through the battle—

Bolstering his allies…

Sowing confusion among their foes.

Arcanus held back, his focus on countering the dark magycks that surged through the stronghold.

With a wave of his staff, he unleashed a torrent of light, dissolving the corruption clinging to the walls and momentarily weakening their enemies.

When the last creature fell, they pressed forward, silent now that they had seen the full horror of Rafe's corruption.

Sorche, ever sharp, whispered, "Any hope to save them after we defeat Rafe?"

Arcanus hesitated.

He wasn't sure.

This… was not part of the plan.

But they were in the thick of it now.

No turning back.

The Inner Sanctum

Navigating the maze-like corridors, the group encountered traps and illusions.

But Arcanus' magyck was strong, and with his team's coordination, they pushed through.

At last, they reached the heart of the fortress.

The inner sanctum.

A massive chamber, its walls etched with intricate sigils that pulsed with eerie light.

Arcanus longed to examine them, to understand their craftsmanship.

But his gaze was drawn to the figure standing in the centre.

Rafe Velisthane.

The once-mighty wizard was stooped over a cane, his frail frame wrapped in loose, tattered robes.

His icy blue eyes, sunken and rimmed with shadow, locked onto Arcanus.

A mixture of defiance and despair.

A Different Kind of Battle

"So, you've come," Rafe rasped, voice brittle.

"The prodigy comes to end what his Elder would not attempt.

How cowardly of my old friend…"

Arcanus raised his staff.

"Your reign of terror ends here, Rafe Velisthane.

The High Council gave you a chance to redeem yourself, and you squandered it.

By their decree, we finish what you started."

He called out a potent retrieval spell.

A spell he had not believed would work.

Until now.

From the depths of the chamber, the Skrol flew into his outstretched hand.

Rafe laughed.

A hollow, bitter sound.

"Redeem myself? Look around you, Arcanus.

Do you see me putting up a fight?

Yes, the fortress was warded. Yes, my guards are twisted mockeries of men.

But it's not what you think."

Arcanus frowned.

There was no resistance.

No mad cackling, no flashing magyck.

Just...

A man broken.

Rafe continued.

"My ambition was my undoing, yes. But I sought to reshape the world, not destroy it as you have heard.

The darkness... it consumed me before I could control it.

It tainted this place. Twisted it.

That is the real danger of dark magyck, Arcanus.

Not that you become corrupted...

But that it has a will of its own."

Berik growled, stepping forward.

"Enough of your excuses. You've caused enough suffering to fill the bellies of a thousand hells!"

Arcanus lowered his staff.

Something felt wrong.

"Wait, Berik."

He studied Rafe closely.

The malevolent aura once wrapped around him…
Had dimmed.
As if the magyck itself had severed its connection.
Rafe's hollow voice filled the chamber.
"I'm dying, Arcanus. Dark magycks need a will devoted to evil.
And since I am no longer that, it has abandoned me.
The black arts have taken everything but my life.
Kill me, and perhaps some of the chaos I unleashed will die with me."
Arcanus hesitated.
Rafe… was telling the truth.
The Shard of Lumina, nestled in his pocket, was a beacon of purity.
A relic said to glow only in the presence of truth.
He brought it out.
It shone brighter than the sun.

A Last Confession

Sorche's voice cut through the silence.
"You expect us to believe you've had a change of heart?
Where is my sister?!"
Rafe's gaze did not waver.
"I swear it upon the Shard Arcanus holds: if you don't believe me, believe the artifact.
Your sister awaits you, Sorche the Enchantress.
She is safe with Berik's Guild of Smithies in the main hall.
I foresaw you would come, and I made the arrangements."
The team halted.
Their weapons half-raised, minds reeling.
Berik's knuckles whitened around his axes.
Sorche's chest rose and fell with short, sharp breaths.

Juju clutched his lute, for once...
Speechless.
Arcanus held Rafe's gaze.
"Then why wait for us?"
Rafe smiled faintly, sadly.
"Because only you can finish this, Arcanus.
Destroy the corruption.
Undo what I could not.
And then... let me rest."
Silence hung thick in the chamber.
The battle wasn't over.
But somehow, Arcanus knew—
The greatest fight lay ahead...

> *"Whoever best describes the problem is the one most likely to solve it."*
>
> *"Improve by 1% a day, and in just 70 days, you're twice as good."*
>
> *"Every successful business (1) creates or provides something of value that (2) other people want or need (3) at a price they're willing to pay, in a way that (4) satisfies the purchaser's needs and expectations and (5) provides the business sufficient revenue to make it worthwhile for the owners to continue operation."*
>
> *"You can't make positive discoveries that make your life better if you never try anything new."*
>
> — Josh Kaufman, The Personal MBA

Arcanus approached Rafe cautiously, his staff glowing brightly as he examined the darkest wizard of their age. Rafe's aura was faint but not malicious— a mixture of green, blue, and white, not the mark of a madman consumed by darkness.

Likewise, the Shard of Lumina resonated with sincerity, confirming Rafe's words as truth.

The voice of the High Elder echoed in Arcanus' mind:

"You can do no more than give someone a second chance, should they be honest in their request.

What say you, Arcanus—does Rafe deserve a second chance?"

Gods, Arcanus hated moments like this.

The kind of decisions that would piss off half the room but needed to be made nonetheless.

He took a breath. "If you are truly sorry for all you have wrought and wish to make amends," Arcanus said, "The High Elder has allowed it, and so it will be done."

"Arcanus, are you mad?" Berik barked. "This man—nay, this unfeeling monster—deserves nothing but death!"

"And what would that accomplish?" Arcanus countered. "Rafe's knowledge could be the key to undoing the damage he's caused. Ending his life now would be a waste, Berik."

Berik growled, swinging his axe at the wall, where it buried itself deep into the stone. "He murdered my family and half my village! How can you expect me to let him go?!"

Arcanus met his friend's furious gaze. "Berik, I cannot tell you to let go of your grief, but I can tell you this—what you're feeling is grief and rage, mostly at yourself. And it is undeserved."

Berik's chest heaved. His expression wavered.

"What do you mean?"

Arcanus' voice was calm, steady. "You're a meticulous planner. A strategic warrior. You have always ensured your village's safety. But that day... the day of the attack—you had a feeling something was off, didn't you?"

Berik's eyes widened, his knuckles tightening around his axe.

"You spoke to your wife about it," Arcanus continued. "You hesitated before leaving for that special cake for your daughter's celebration. You told yourself you were overthinking things, that you'd hurry back. And you left."

A shuddering breath left Berik's lips.

"For all your planning, for all your sense of responsibility—that was the first day in your life you felt you failed. But hear me, Berik.

There was nothing you could do. Nothing to plan for. Nothing to control. You could not have changed the outcome."

Berik's eyes filled with tears, his axe slipping from his grip as he fell to his knees.

"I was not there... I was not there..."

Arcanus nodded, sorrowful but unwavering. "I know it doesn't make the pain go away. But when tragedy strikes, our minds scramble for control, for blame. The truth is, sometimes life happens, and no amount of preparation can stop it.

Be kind to yourself, my friend. As kind as you would be to another in your shoes."

Juju, humming a gentle, mournful tune, knelt beside Berik, offering silent comfort.

The Oracle Awakens

Arcanus turned back to the ancient Skrol in his hands, its power thrumming through his veins.

Taking a deep breath, he raised his staff and channelled his magyck.

The chamber flared with an otherworldly light as the Skrol

and staff merged, their combined energy pulsing outward in waves of pure white radiance.

The light condensed, twisting into a brilliant, floating sphere.

Then—

A voice echoed through the chamber.

"You have summoned me, human. Pray tell, why?"

They all stared.

Even Berik froze, his sorrow momentarily forgotten.

Juju gasped. "Oh golly, the light is talking!"

Arcanus ignored him. "Purest of energies, who are you? What do I call you?"

The sphere pulsed. "You may call me Oracle."

"Oracle," Arcanus said carefully, "I face a conundrum unlike any other. My plans have unravelled; the path twisted into something I never foresaw. I do not know what to do."

The Oracle hummed. "You wish to absolve the fallen wizard. Do you believe he deserves mercy?"

"I do not know," Arcanus admitted. "I cannot see what the future holds. But I also do not wish to be the cause of another's death."

The Oracle's light flickered. "And yet, you came prepared to fight to the death, did you not?"

Arcanus hesitated.

"I never intended to kill Rafe," he confessed. "I meant to place him in stasis, to be held within the Arcane Academy's vault. But I admit... it was a risky plan."

The Oracle pulsed, turning toward Berik.

"You are a curious species, humans. So many would have taken life without a second thought, were it required. Would you not, warrior?"

Berik's red-rimmed eyes met the entity's glow. He said nothing.

"I will assist you, Arcanus," the Oracle declared. "In return, you will do something for me."

Arcanus nodded. "Name it."

The light engulfed Rafe, a brilliant wave of purification spreading across the chamber.

The fortress shuddered as the corruption peeled away.

Rafe staggered, his form growing stronger, more stable.

When the light faded, the Oracle whispered in Arcanus' mind:

"Take me home, human. Take me to the Temple of the Ancients in Raghan."

The light condensed into a crystalline diamond, warm to the touch.

Arcanus placed it carefully inside his robes.

Rafe, standing taller now, reached for the Lumina Shard.

It flared bright as he swore his oath.

"I will make this right," Rafe said. "You have my word."

New Beginnings

In the Great Hall, Sorche's sister, Isla, greeted them with joyful tears.

The monstrous beings of the fortress had returned to their original forms, their memories wiped of their time as Rafe's twisted soldiers.

Berik's warrior guild welcomed him home, offering him the role of Commander of New Recruits.

Juju somehow convinced both Sorche and Isla to work for him—one as his talent manager, the other as his costume designer.

Arcanus smiled, heart full.

As he turned to leave, Berik approached. "I hope you know what you're doing."

Arcanus grinned, gripping his friend's forearm. "I suppose we'll find out."

He watched as Rafe stepped through the glowing blue portal, vanishing into the Arcane Academy's hold.

His path was set.

But Arcanus had one last task.

He touched the Oracle's crystal in his pocket.

The road to Raghan awaited.

And maybe, just maybe—

He'd take the scenic route.

EDICTS OF THE WISE
Planning and Accountability: The Foundation of Leadership

Planning is Non-Negotiable

No matter how unpredictable things get, planning is what prepares you for success. Your plan might not survive reality—things will shift, priorities will change, and challenges will arise. But without a plan, you're flying blind. The process of planning is what matters most. It forces you to think ahead, spot risks, and set a clear direction. That's what allows you to adapt quickly when things don't go as expected.

Execution Beats Endless Planning—Get Moving

A plan that never gets executed is just a theory with good intentions. Over-planning kills momentum. Some leaders obsess over refining every detail but never actually pull the trigger. Perfect plans don't exist—execution and adaptation do. Build a solid plan, then start. Adjust as needed, but don't mistake endless preparation for progress. Nothing happens until you make it happen.

Know Your Tools: Project Management Methods Matter

Different projects need different approaches. Understanding methodologies like Waterfall, PMBOK, and Agile gives you the flexibility to apply the right tool for the job.

- » Waterfall brings structure and predictability.
- » PMBOK provides a complete framework for managing projects from start to finish.
- » Agile thrives in fast-moving, changing environments where flexibility is key.
- » And many more

Smart leaders don't get stuck on one method. They learn the strengths of each and use the right one when needed.

Cut the Noise—Deliver Value

Cut out anything that doesn't add real value. If something isn't driving progress, get rid of it. Don't waste time on pointless tasks or busywork just to feel productive. It's easy to mistake movement for progress, but they are not the same. If it's not moving the team forward, or the results of the team, drop it.

Failure will happen, and that's okay. What matters is how you respond to it. When failure happens (because it will, and IT WILL), take the lesson, adjust, and go again. Learn, refine, and keep improving. Break work into small, clear steps so you can iterate rather than waiting for perfection. The goal isn't to get everything right the first time—it's to keep getting better every time. Progress beats perfection.

OKRs Keep Teams Focused and Accountable

Objectives and Key Results (OKRs) are one of the best ways to stay focused on what truly matters. Every person and every team should be aligned to measurable outcomes that contribute to the bigger mission. OKRs provide:

- » Clear expectations
- » A way to measure progress
- » Accountability without micromanagement

OKRs let people own their work. They show their results instead of waiting to be asked. Used properly, they drive action, clarity, and impact.

Accountability Should Never Be Shared

If more than one person is accountable, no one is accountable. When ownership is spread too thin, things slip through the cracks. Decisions are delayed. Performance suffers.

One person must own each task, goal, or outcome. That doesn't mean working alone—collaboration is essential. But at the end of the day, there should always be one person responsible for seeing it through.

Accountability Drives Performance

When people take ownership, they become more engaged, more proactive, and more invested. A culture of accountability makes teams stronger. It pushes people to grow, refine their skills, and raise their standards.

A high-performing team isn't just a group of skilled individuals—it's a unit where:

- » Everyone understands their role
- » People deliver on their commitments
- » Colleagues trust each other to follow through

This level of discipline in execution is what separates average teams from truly great ones.

Stay in Your Lane: Work at the Right Level

When people focus on their core responsibilities, teams become more efficient. Work gets done by the right people at the right time. It removes friction, eliminates confusion, and keeps things running smoothly.

Leaders should not micromanage. Stay at the right level—support, guide, and set direction, but let people do their jobs.

Accountability Creates Job Satisfaction

People don't burn out from hard work. They burn out from chaos, lack of direction, and unclear expectations.

When expectations are clear, when people see their impact, and when they take ownership of results, work becomes rewarding. People thrive in environments where their contributions matter.

Projects Need Structure: Think in Programs, Not Just Tasks

A list of projects isn't just separate tasks—together, they form a program. Programs align work, manage resources, and create bigger impact.

Leaders don't just oversee projects—they connect the dots. They ensure everything moves toward a common goal.

Even business-as-usual (BAU) activities should be treated with structure. Ongoing operations need leadership and accountability, just like projects do. Programs keep everything focused, efficient, and connected to the bigger picture.

OKRs Must Be Actively Led

OKRs aren't just goals—they drive action and results. Leaders must embed them into daily work, keep teams aligned, and hold people accountable.

Leadership in this space means removing blockers and keeping key results front and centre in decision-making.

Master Prioritisation and Delegation

Not all tasks are equal. The Eisenhower Matrix is a powerful tool to separate urgent vs. important work.

- » Urgent & Important? Do it now.
- » Important but Not Urgent? Plan for it.

- » Urgent but Not Important? Delegate it.
- » Neither? Drop it.

Great leaders focus on what moves the needle.

Delegation is a Leadership Skill

Delegation isn't offloading work. It's about:

- » Empowering people
- » Building capability
- » Ensuring the right people are doing the right things

The best leaders set clear expectations, provide support, and hold people accountable for results. They trust their team but stay aware of progress.

Done well, delegation elevates both the leader and the team.

Set Teams Up for Success

Setting ambitious goals isn't enough. Leaders must ensure their teams have:

- » The right tools
- » The right skills
- » The right support

That means:

- » Securing budget
- » Providing training
- » Removing obstacles

Leadership isn't about pushing harder; it's about creating an environment where success is possible.

Leading Multiple Programs Requires Strategic Thinking

Managing multiple programs isn't about juggling tasks—it's about shaping strategic direction. Success isn't just hitting individual project milestones—it's about aligning everything to bigger business goals.

They zoom out to see the big picture, while still handling the details that drive execution.

True Leadership Means True Ownership

Ownership isn't just about one project or department—it extends across the entire business.

Think of it like a Venn diagram—each team has its own priorities, but leaders exist in the overlapping space. They ensure alignment, remove roadblocks, and connect teams to drive progress.

True ownership means working across functions to make things happen. It's about:

- » Influence
- » Trust
- » Collaboration

Great leaders don't just manage their team—they help the whole organisation succeed.

Accountability and Performance Go Hand in Hand

A team's performance level shapes how goals should be set and accountability structured.

- » High-performing teams operate in environments where the stakes are high—whether due to market competition, innovation demands, or rapid execution requirements. In these settings, failure to deliver has tangible consequences, making urgency and excellence non-negotiable. These teams thrive on ambitious targets, autonomy, and a fast-paced rhythm that challenges them to push boundaries and continuously improve.

- » In contrast, low-performing teams exist in environments where there are fewer immediate consequences for underperformance. This is often the case in bureaucratic organisations or monopolies, where goals can be adjusted with little impact, and a culture of complacency can take root. These teams require stronger leadership intervention, clear direction, and often a shift in mindset to drive meaningful progress. Simply increasing expectations without addressing the underlying issues won't create improvement. It takes a combination of structure, accountability, and cultural change.

- » Medium-performing teams fall somewhere in between. They may be functional but not exceptional, needing targeted guidance, skill development, and a clear framework for success.

One-size-fits-all leadership doesn't work. The best leaders assess performance levels and adjust their approach:

- » Push high performers to innovate.
- » Provide structure for mid-level teams.
- » Intervene and set stronger accountability for low-performing teams.

The key is to maintain accountability at every level while ensuring growth and continuous improvement.

Meetings Are a Cost—Use Them Wisely

Meetings aren't free. They cost time, focus, and energy—and if they're not driving decisions or clearing roadblocks, they're just noise. If something can be solved with an email, a Slack message, or a quick one-on-one, do that instead. Treat meetings like an investment and make sure they pay big dividends. If you're sitting in meetings all day, you're not leading—you're just talking about leading.

Focus on What Achieves the Result—Not Just Looking Busy

Productivity isn't the goal—getting the result is. Too many teams burn time on admin work, status updates, and process for the sake of process. Looking busy means nothing if it doesn't drive real progress. The best teams cut distractions, focus on the highest-impact work, and make sure every effort gets them closer to success. Stop glorifying being busy and start making moves that matter.

Side Quest
The Overturned Wagon

The road was quiet as Arcanus and his companions approached an overturned wagon. The narrow pathway was completely blocked, supplies and artifacts scattered across the dirt. Scrolls, glowing crystals, and a peculiar stone tablet engraved with stick-figure diagrams lay in disarray. At the centre of the mess, a goblin with oversized spectacles and a crooked tie sat, furiously scribbling notes onto a parchment while muttering to himself.

Arcanus stepped forward, his staff glowing faintly in the twilight—a curious reaction. "Trouble, traveller?" he asked.

The goblin groaned and gestured wildly at the chaotic scene before him. "It's everything! The starstone project, the rune restoration initiative, the Flamewood revival—all delayed! My resources are scattered, my priorities are tangled, and the council insists I deliver all results yesterday! It's like trying to wrangle a pack of feral kobolds with a wet rope."

Arcanus knelt, picking up the engraved tablet. It depicted crude, pointy-haired goblins holding meeting stones labelled "synergy" and "actionable steps." He arched an eyebrow. "This wouldn't happen to be the Parchment to Program Management, would it?"

The goblin let out an exasperated sigh. "Yes, and it's useless! None of it works in real life."

Suppressing a chuckle, Arcanus tapped his staff on the ground, conjuring a shimmering grid in the air. "Your tasks are like this matrix. Focus on what's vital first. Delegate the rest to those you trust—or kobolds, if they're feeling cooperative…"

Under Arcanus' guidance, the team organised the goblin's tasks. Berik hauled the heavy starstones and repaired the wagon. Sorche mapped a path to nearby allies who could assist. Juju, meanwhile, hopped from one person to the next, singing enthusiastically—though in truth, doing little beyond boosting morale.

The goblin, watching the order emerge from the chaos, rubbed the back of his neck sheepishly. "I've been so focused on juggling everything that I actually forgot to prioritise."

Arcanus smiled, handing the goblin the tablet. "Even in chaos, clarity is possible. But remember—no guide can fix poor execution. Not even if the goblin on the cover has pointy hair."

The goblin snorted with laughter. "That's fair, wise mage. And thanks for fixing my mess."

As the goblin trundled off, tie flapping in the wind, Sorche turned to Arcanus with an amused smirk. "Pointy-haired goblin, huh?"

Arcanus chuckled. "I hear they're notoriously difficult to work for."

With that, he signalled to the others. "Let's move—we have little time."

"I can't believe it! Reading and writing actually paid off!"

— The Simpsons, Season 3, Episode 2

"Weaseling out of things is what separates us from the animals. Except the weasel."

— The Simpsons, Season 5, Episode 8

Side Quest
Commanding the Winds

Many many more moons ago

The mountain wind howled as Arcanus stood at the edge of the ridge, staring down at the ruined watchtower of Sŭl, its crumbling form flickering with faint blue light. Legend held that the artifact inside could calm the storms that plagued the pass, but reaching it—and activating it—would demand every ounce of teamwork and grit from the mismatched group at his back. He had argued with the High Elder that the mission's success would be greater if he could choose his own team, but the High Elder had dismissed the notion. So here they were.

Turning to the assembled crew, his cloak snapping in the wind, Arcanus surveyed them with a critical eye. "This mission has three parts," he said. "Fynn, you take your team and clear the rubble. Gella, your group secures the tower—keep it standing while the artifact wakes up. Torren…" He paused, looking at the young mage and his nervous recruits. "You're on artifact activation. It's the most dangerous job, but it's why you're here. If we don't get this done, well, let's just say the High Elder is going to be PO'd big time."

Torren shifted uneasily. "What if we can't do it? I mean, what if—"

"You'll figure it out," Arcanus interrupted, his tone firm but reassuring. "This artifact controls storms. If you don't succeed, none of us leave this mountain. Trust your team, lead like it matters—because it does." A faint smile tugged at his lips. "And remember: make it so."

The teams scattered, disappearing into the roaring storm. Hours passed as Arcanus moved between them, offering steady guidance and encouragement. He hauled stones alongside Fynn's crew, gave Gella's group advice on reinforcing the structure, and stood with Torren's team as they faced the pulsating artifact. Every piece had to come together—every person had to own their part if the mission was to succeed.

Finally, with a deafening hum, the artifact blazed to life. The storm broke, the skies cleared, and the team regrouped around the tower, breathless but triumphant.

"You did it!" Arcanus called, his voice carrying over the now-calm mountain air. "Not because I told you how, but because you found the way and pushed through. That's the only thing that matters out here."

As the crew began their descent, Torren caught up to him, grinning. "I guess leadership is more than barking orders, eh, Arcanus?"

Arcanus chuckled. "It's about knowing when to step in—and when to let others rise to the challenge." He glanced back at the glowing artifact, then down at the winding trail ahead. "Now let's move. The next storm won't wait forever..."

THE UNWRITTEN RULES

Progress Over Perfection—Keep Moving Forward

It's easy to get lost in the details, refining and reworking something until it feels perfect. But perfection isn't the goal—progress is. The best way to get things done is to focus on what's "good enough" to move forward, rather than what's flawless. If a task is 80% ready and that's enough to take the next step, take it. Prioritise momentum over endless tweaking—progress comes from action, not just refinement.

Directness is Good—But Delivery Shapes the Response

Being clear and direct is a strength, especially when setting expectations. But tone and wording affect how people receive the message. Not everyone hears what was meant—they hear how it was said. Instead of "You didn't meet the deadline," saying "I noticed the deadline was missed—what do you need to get back on track?" keeps accountability strong without creating unnecessary tension. Directness lands best when it's paired with clarity and a problem-solving approach.

People Commit More to Plans They Help Build

Accountability works best when people feel a sense of ownership over their work. Instead of assigning tasks like a checklist, engage them in the process:

"How do you see this fitting into our objectives?" or "What do you need to make this successful?" When people feel part of the decision-making process, they're far more likely to follow through and take responsibility rather than just comply with instructions.

Delegation is About Clarity and Trust

Delegation isn't just about handing off work—it's about trusting people while giving them the structure they need to succeed. Instead of "Here, just do this," try:

"I trust you to handle this—let me know if you hit any roadblocks or if you need anything extra." This sets a clear expectation while allowing autonomy. People thrive when they know what's expected, what success looks like, and where they can ask for support. Clear ownership + clear support = real results.

THE MIRROR OF MASTERY

» What specific challenges do I face when I don't plan ahead, and how do they affect my ability to achieve what matters most?

» When I commit to something and follow through, how does it shape the way others see me, and how does it make me feel about myself?

» If I had a step-by-step plan and a way to track my progress, how much easier would it be to stay focused, and how would I ensure I stick to it?

A GILDED EDGE

When working within a structured plan or accountability framework (such as OKRs or the Eisenhower Matrix), how do you balance the need for clear, direct expectations with the inevitable uncertainty and ambiguity that comes with leadership?

In a leadership role, how do you ensure accountability—both for yourself and for others—without micromanaging or overwhelming your team?

How do you determine when to take ownership versus when to delegate, and how do you make sure those you delegate to have the resources and clarity they need to succeed?

The Eisenhower Matrix, also known as the Urgent-Important Matrix, is a decision-making framework that helps prioritise tasks based on urgency and importance. It consists of four quadrants:

Urgent & Important (Do Now) – Tasks that require immediate attention and have significant consequences if not completed (e.g., crises, deadlines, urgent problems).

Important but Not Urgent (Plan) – Tasks that contribute to long-term success but don't require immediate action (e.g., strategic planning, skill-building, relationship development).

Urgent but Not Important (Delegate) – Tasks that demand immediate attention but don't contribute significantly to goals (e.g., interruptions, routine emails, meetings that others can handle).

Neither Urgent Nor Important (Eliminate) – Tasks that add little to no value and should be minimised or removed (e.g., excessive social media, busywork, distractions).

By categorising tasks using this matrix, leaders and teams can focus on what truly matters, delegate effectively, and reduce time wasted on low-value activities.

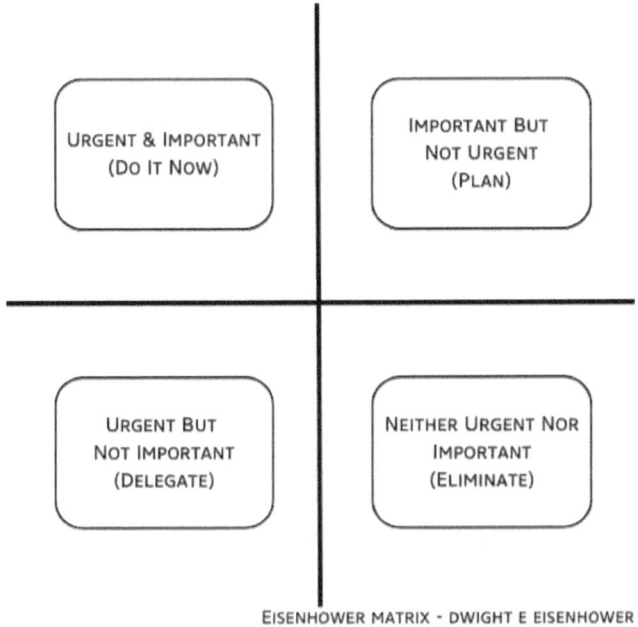

EISENHOWER MATRIX - DWIGHT E EISENHOWER

CHAPTER 8

The Mantle of Trust and Counsel

Main Quest

The Odyssey of Purposeful Leadership

Two weeks later

Arcanus wondered what his friends were up to as he spent his second full week navigating Raghan. For all its starkness, there was a certain beauty laid bare in the dunes, and from what the Oracle had imparted, the place they were heading to was something of an oasis. He had left his horse with Berik, entrusting him to see to his steed until he returned. He knew the fastest way to travel the desert was on a sand rider, a vehicle not unlike a boat with a sail, designed to glide speedily over sand.

The rider itself had a beautiful and clever design, with a steering wheel that controlled the sail in whichever direction one wished to go. Its polished copper and mahogany features gleamed in the sunlight as the black sail caught the frequent gusts of wind, propelling it forward at great speeds. The extra-wide skids beneath the vehicle, a feature the salesman had assured him he would be grateful for "once you're actually stuck in it," proved extremely handy. The ride was almost effortless, thanks to the anti-friction charm he had cast upon it.

As the wind howled around him, Arcanus pulled his cloak tighter and adjusted his goggles, grateful for the protection both provided. He had enchanted his cloak with a cooling charm to combat the desert's brutal heat, and he was thankful for his sharp skills in spells, charms, and potions. This heat was a killer, and as a non-native to the desert, he could have succumbed to heat sickness many times over the past two weeks. He was comfortable enough for the moment—except for the rash that had now spread all over his body. None of his usual spells or potions had provided any relief.

His hand drifted to the concealed pocket over his heart, where he felt the comforting weight of the diamond resting against his chest. It was an honour to transport the mythic Oracle home, after all, it had been missing for several centuries, and no one had truly understood where the being had disappeared to. Reflecting on the Oracle, Arcanus realised he would likely become a target if word got out that he carried the source of all wisdom and knowledge.

Once, the Oracle's advice had been sought by kings and peasants, scholars and adventurers alike; the price of its wisdom? The treacherous journey across the desert. Only those with the courage and fortitude to traverse the harsh dunes, facing extreme heat by day and freezing cold by night, were deemed worthy. In a way, it made sense—nothing good ever came easy, and if one wished for wisdom from the best, they had to prove themselves up to the task. They had to show they were mature enough to handle the advice that was gifted to them.

Arcanus was unsure of the final resting place of the Oracle. His last communication with the High Elder had confirmed it lay somewhere in an oasis, but little else was known. It could just as easily be an underground cavern or a temple worthy of the ancient gods. Regardless, it was a once-in-a-lifetime experience, and he had been entrusted with the stone. A surge of pride filled him. He was trusted. A low-born human elevated to the ranks of trusted advisor by the High Council.

The ever-present rash itched near the arch of his foot, and

he gritted his teeth in frustration. "Only a few more days, and I'll be free to deal with this irritation," he muttered into the wind.

The copper compass, inlaid in the middle of the steering wheel, pointed due north, and he could tell by the shadows over the dunes that he was making good time. As he crested a massive dune, movement caught his eye—a hand waving furiously. Arcanus lifted his own hand in acknowledgment. Travelers. He had seen several over the last two weeks—the desert held an ancient, mysterious beauty, and wanderers were not uncommon.

Thinking he could push further before making camp, he continued on—perhaps further than he should have. At some point, exhaustion claimed him, and he fell asleep at the helm. When he startled awake, he found the rider had stopped, pressing against something half-buried in the sand. The sun had long dipped below the horizon, and the night sky stretched vast above him, showered in a million twinkling stars.

Setting the brakes, he climbed down, groaning as he stretched out his tired limbs.

With efficient precision, he set up camp, erecting the canopy and laying out his bedroll alongside a small clockwork lantern, its soft amber glow casting a warm light over his temporary home. It made for a cosy picture, a small island of warmth in the cold desert night.

The Oracle pulsed warmly against his chest, almost as though it were… alive. He pulled it free and held it up to the lantern's glow, watching as prismatic colours scattered through the diamond's flawless surface. Nature was truly a wonder.

Like himself, the diamond had undergone extreme pressure, yet emerged stronger. He could only hope he had a similar destiny.

Twelve hours later

Arcanus knew they had arrived. He could feel it. The energy pulsing from the Diamond had grown stronger, a steady thump every few seconds, as if it had a heartbeat of its own. He pulled off his goggles, shading his eyes with one hand as he scanned the endless desert horizon. At first glance, there seemed to be nothing—only dunes stretching endlessly under the golden sun. But he could feel something.

Magyck was alive here. Present. Waiting.

Dismounting from the sand rider, Arcanus landed lightly on the ground, the sand shifting beneath his boots. He murmured the words to a reveal spell and waited. Nothing. The desert remained still, silent save for the whispering wind.

The Diamond thumped harder against his chest. Calling.

With a slow breath, he pulled it free from his pocket, its flawless surface shimmering in the midday light. Why not? He performed the spell again, this time holding the Diamond in his palm.

A brilliant burst of light erupted around him, and suddenly, the air shimmered like the surface of a mirage. Shapes blurred and twisted, then solidified before his eyes.

The oasis was revealing itself.

It must have sensed the Oracle's return.

Arcanus stepped forward carefully, the shifting illusion now giving way to lush greenery, a pristine pool of sapphire water, and—robed figures moving between the trees. He stilled, surprised. Monks. He had not expected this.

The Oracle pulsed warmly in his hand as he approached one of the figures. The monk turned, their expression calm but knowing, as if they had been expecting him.

"We have waited," the monk said simply. "It was foretold that one would bring the Oracle home."

Arcanus absorbed this information silently. Foretold? He had not been made aware of any prophecy, but if they had been guarding this place for centuries, then this was truly where the Oracle was meant to rest.

With quiet reverence, he followed the monk deeper into the temple, its massive doors carved with intricate reliefs depicting the history of Ez, the Kingdom of Naivohw, and the other great cities he had recently visited. His fingers brushed lightly over the detailed carvings, and in that moment, a surge of power shot through him.

He inhaled sharply. Unusual.

Inside, the temple was just as breathtaking. The timeless architecture seamlessly blended crystal, brass, and iron, giving it an ancient yet strangely modern appearance. Metal and copper pipes twisted along the walls, almost as if guided by the glowing runes embedded beneath them.

At the centre of it all stood a great chamber, its walls formed from a type of crystal Arcanus had never seen before. The light within refracted in mesmerising hues, illuminating an emerald pedestal at its heart.

He knew immediately.

This was where the Diamond was meant to rest.

The monks gathered in a silent circle, their robes whispering against the stone floor. The leader stepped forward, bowing low before extending his hands toward the Oracle. Arcanus hesitated for only a moment before carefully placing it in the monk's waiting hands.

With a steady grace, the monk turned and gently lowered the Diamond onto the pedestal.

And as it touched the smooth emerald surface, the chamber blazed with light.

> *"The most effective way to influence a client is to help the person feel that the solution was (to a large extent) his or her idea, or at the very least, his or her decision."*
>
> *"It is not enough for a professional to be right: An advisor's job is to be helpful."*
>
> *"People don't care what you know until they know that you care."*
>
> *"The ability to establish, grow, extend, and restore trust is the key skill of the new economy."*
>
> *"The key to professional success is not just technical mastery of one's discipline... but also the ability to work with clients in such a way as to earn their trust and gain their confidence."*
>
> — David H. Maister, Charles H. Green, and Robert M. Galford, **The Trusted Advisor**

The head monk regarded Arcanus with solemn gratitude. "You have done us a great service, one which cannot be repaid in all likelihood."

Arcanus inclined his head, his voice steady but warm. "It was an honour to bring the great wisdom back home." When they invited him to stay, he readily accepted. After everything he had been through, a period of rest and reflection was exactly what he needed.

Over the next couple of months, he grew familiar with the monks and their way of life, and they, in turn, grew to know him. They were a dedicated order, unwavering in their commitment to serve those in need. However, Arcanus soon noticed a troubling pattern—petty thefts were increasing around the oasis. A suspicion grew in his mind: was this how the Oracle had been lost in the first place?

That evening, seemingly by coincidence, the head monk invited Arcanus to attend their monthly meeting.

"Arcanus," the elder began, his hands clasped before him, "we have been facing a dilemma. On one hand, we are committed to aiding the less fortunate. On the other, we cannot allow a repeat of the tragedy that saw the Oracle stolen. We must find a way to serve the community while protecting the Oasis, the Temple, and the Oracle."

Arcanus nodded, appreciating the trust it took for them to include him in such discussions. He listened carefully as the monks outlined their security setup—it all seemed fairly standard at first, but as they spoke, he realised something crucial.

Their wards were incredibly powerful.

This, ironically, was the root of their problem. The wards were attracting individuals sensitive to magyckal energy—people seeking to exploit its power.

The question was, how to explain this without directly saying it?

Arcanus leaned forward slightly. "Tell me, old one, how did you come to be a guardian of the Temple?"

The head monk nodded thoughtfully and gestured for him to sit upon a comfortable dais before answering.

"Not all who prepare for monkhood pass the test," the elder explained. "It takes years of study and sacrifice. It is a hereditary path—my father, my grandfather, and my ancestors going back a millennia have been honoured to serve. For me, it was natural. Being accepted into the order was the greatest honour of my life."

Arcanus could hear the undercurrent of pride and pain in his voice. He remained silent, waiting for the monk to continue.

"Around a century ago, a deadly sandstorm struck the oasis. Our wards usually protect us from such disasters, but this storm felt different—as though driven by magyckal forces. When we finally made it back to the Temple, we discovered a terrible truth." The monk's voice grew heavy. "The Oracle's body had been destroyed, and its vessel—the diamond you carried here—was missing."

Arcanus listened intently as the elder continued.

"The Oracle's energy is sentient. It understood that the thief intended to misuse its power, so it fractured itself, splitting into two magyckal artifacts. Those fragments found their way to your wizarding academy, locked away by the High Elders, waiting for a soul worthy of restoring them."

The monk looked at Arcanus with profound respect. "Had the magyckal parchment not gone missing, the Oracle may have remained lost forever." He took a deep breath. "To be chosen as guardians of the Oracle is an honour. To have failed in our duty was our greatest shame. You have restored our honour by returning the great enlightenment of the ages."

Arcanus was glad to have helped them regain their sense of purpose. But now, they needed to find a lasting solution—together.

A young monk raised a hand. "What if we set up perimeter barriers several miles away? We could keep negative elements from entering the area altogether."

The monks erupted in chatter, some agreeing, others protesting.

"No, we are here to help! Not everyone is without sin. We'd be turning away people who may have made mistakes but still need guidance."

Ideas flew back and forth, yet none seemed ideal.

Arcanus let the discussion unfold before speaking. "I see you have a battalion of trained guards. What role do they play when you already have such powerful wards in place?"

The monks turned toward the guards standing at a respectful distance and nodded in understanding.

The head monk explained their role: "They are trained in combat and security. Their task is to physically defend the Temple and oasis. We use magyck only as a last resort…"

As he spoke the words aloud, Arcanus could see realisation dawn across several faces.

The first line of defence was not the guards—it was the wards.

They had inadvertently turned their Temple into a beacon, drawing in those seeking to exploit its power.

"So, your goal is…?" Arcanus prompted.

The monks conferred among themselves before one spoke up. "To serve the community while ensuring the Temple, Oasis, and Oracle remain safe."

Arcanus nodded. "And your resources?"

A young monk suddenly stood, his eyes bright with inspiration. "Let's examine the manpower the Temple has at its disposal."

Another voice picked up the idea and ran with it. "Wait! What if we removed the wards from the templ—"

An uproar erupted.

The head monk raised a hand for silence, motioning for the speaker to continue.

"If we remove the wards from the Temple, it will no longer be a beacon luring thieves and scoundrels. Instead, we use the guards as the first line of defence."

A murmur of agreement rippled through the chamber.

"Yes," another monk chimed in. "We already train the guards rigorously. They are meant to protect us, yet we have been relying on magyck instead of them."

Arcanus observed the growing consensus and smiled.

"This solution allows you to remain true to your mission," he said. "You continue serving those in need without attracting the wrong kind of attention. The guards uphold their purpose, and the community remains protected."

The head monk folded his hands, deep in thought, then slowly nodded. "We need to refine the details, but I believe this is the balance we have sought for so long."

Arcanus leaned back slightly, pleased with their progress. "Then let's get to work."

> "The only way to influence people is to talk in terms of what the other person wants."
>
> "To be interesting, be interested."
>
> "Criticism is dangerous, because it wounds a person's precious pride, hurts his sense of importance, and arouses resentment."
>
> "When dealing with people, remember you are not dealing with creatures of logic, but with creatures bristling with prejudice and motivated by pride and vanity."
>
> — Dale Carnegie,
> How to Win Friends and Influence People for the Digital Era

Arcanus stepped forward once more, his gaze thoughtful as he considered their discussions. "Hmm... you are dedicating a large amount of resources to the wards."

He let the statement hang in the air, allowing the monks

to process the weight of his words. Slowly, he watched the head monk's expression shift—realisation dawning like the morning sun.

"Yes! That's perfect," the elder monk exclaimed. "If we ward each guard individually with a small amount of energy, we can maintain the protection of the wards without attracting unwanted elements the way a massive forcefield does!"

A wave of excitement and relief spread through the gathered monks. Some murmured in agreement, while others nodded enthusiastically at the simplicity and effectiveness of the plan.

The head monk turned to Arcanus, his wise eyes filled with approval. "I spoke with your High Elder not long ago, and he assured me that you were a bright and resourceful fellow. I see now that despite your young age in wizarding years, he was absolutely correct."

Arcanus grinned, feeling a sense of satisfaction settle within him. For once, there was nothing else to do but enjoy the moment.

Several days later

Arcanus sat among the monks, listening intently as they spoke of the rituals and legacy surrounding the Oracle's existence.

"The souls that house the Oracle must be tempered and wise," the head monk explained. "They must have no personal ambitions for great gain and be humble to their core. Essentially, we have curated these souls for the Oracle, as such qualities are almost impossible to find within a single being. Unfortunately, once the Oracle lay dormant in those artifacts, our temple and everything within fell into stasis, disappearing into time."

Arcanus' astonishment must have been evident, because

the head monk offered him an understanding smile. "Yes, I am roughly one hundred and fifty years old, but not by choice."

Arcanus hesitated before asking the one question that gnawed at his mind. "Why do you think the Oracle decided to reveal itself at this particular time?"

The head monk studied him for a long moment before clearing his throat. A strange warmth spread through Arcanus—not from the desert heat, not even from his cursed rash, but something deeper, something unknown.

"We have consulted with the Gods for several weeks now. Once we knew the Oracle was returning home, we asked our Seer to harvest all the information about the stone carrier—about you."

Arcanus felt his stomach drop. "Me?"

"Yes, you, Arcanus Mylar." The monk's voice was calm but weighted. "Born into a minor noble family that lacked wealth and influence, you were always treated as an outsider, despite your natural gift for leadership and intuition. You fought for the greater good, never seeking to lord over others, and this made you unique—someone who had the ability to possess real power but never abuse it. You endured and sought to better yourself not for selfish gain, but to serve others. You do not command through intimidation or entitlement, but through quiet determination, guiding others to do better.

Even now, your assistance with the wards and the thefts has highlighted who and what you are. You placed no demands upon us, nor did you dictate terms. You merely showed the way, and in doing so, allowed the brotherhood to find their own path. Your essence, your soul, speaks with clarity, wisdom, and compassion—and the Oracle stone has responded."

A sharp breath left Arcanus, and something deep inside

him cracked open. He felt tears well in his eyes, emotions rushing through him in waves—honour, humility, disbelief.

"To be the Oracle is to bear responsibility," the monk continued. "To trust in yourself, to know that your words and thoughts come not from arrogance, but from experience, from humility, from compassion—a balanced view that takes everything into account.

The choice is yours to make."

And then, one by one, the monks departed, leaving Arcanus alone.

For a brief moment, he felt bereft, untethered.

And yet, it made sense. Like everything in his life had been leading to this very moment. Every challenge, every lesson, every sacrifice.

But could he truly go through with it?

The faces of his friends flickered in his mind—Berik, ever steadfast. Sorche, sharp-witted and bold. Juju, ridiculous yet irreplaceable. He thought of the Arcane Academy, the High Elder, the comforts of his simple room, his beloved horse...

And then, a hysterical laugh bubbled up within him.

This was a real kicker. Arcanus Mylar—once a minor noble with nothing to his name—now stood at the precipice of becoming the highest authority in the world.

An hour later

Arcanus stood in the great chamber, his breath steady as he prepared for what was to come. The cleansing ritual was complete, and before him, the head monk lifted the Diamond from its pedestal, his lips moving in a chant too low to hear.

As the chanting intensified, the Diamond dissolved into shimmering motes of light, and from it, the being made of pure energy reemerged—radiant, ancient, eternal.

"We meet again, Arcanus," the Oracle intoned, its voice echoing through the chamber, a thousand voices speaking as one. "I had a feeling it would be you…"

Arcanus bowed his head, drawing in a slow, measured breath. He closed his eyes, centring himself as the chanting grew louder, reverberating through his very bones.

And then, he felt it—the Oracle moving closer, its energy like fire and ice, life and death, everything and nothing all at once.

A violent shudder ripped through his body. He felt like he was being unmade, his soul stretched across the universe, seeing and feeling everything within the span of a heartbeat. Time lost meaning. Thought became weightless.

Then, silence.

The storm within him settled, the chaos balanced itself, and he was whole again—but different.

Arcanus opened his eyes, feeling endless. He was still himself, yet more. Power pulsed through his veins, not as a force to wield, but as an intrinsic part of existence itself. He understood everything, all at once, yet with the clarity of a still mind.

Across the world, the High Elder gazed into the Seeing Stone, watching in silent joy. He had known this moment would come, and a single tear slipped down his lined cheek.

A wizard could ask for no greater honour than to have one of their own become the Oracle.

With his newfound sight, Arcanus turned his gaze outward, searching for the ones he loved.

He found Sorche, Isla, and Juju, traveling in splendid style to Juju's next grand performance. Sorche had fully embraced her role as Juju's manager and protector, and Juju's aura—once tinged with sadness—now glowed a brilliant yellow, radiant with joy.

Next, he searched for Berik—and what he saw warmed his heart.

Berik, ever the warrior, had finally found peace. He stood before a young boy, an orphan he had taken in as his own. Arcanus smiled. Berik had always had a wealth of love to give—he just needed someone to give it to.

Finally, he turned his attention to Rafe.

What he saw surprised him—yet, at the same time, it didn't.

Rafe had kept his word. More than that, he was actively making amends, seeking out every person whose life had been affected by his actions. In time, within a decade, he would be offered a seat on the High Council.

And despite his hesitation, the High Elder would urge him to accept.

"For all the good you've done," he would tell him.

With that final vision, Arcanus knew his mission was complete.

It was a bittersweet moment.

Finally, he turned his gaze inward, seeing himself as he now was. He still bore his own essence, his own spirit, yet he had changed.

His once-dark hair had become a flowing mane of white, gleaming like moonlight woven into silk. His eyes—once a deep brown—were now silver, reflecting the wisdom of the ages.

He blinked, tilting his head slightly, and noticed something peculiar.

The rash.

It was gone.

Arcanus let out a breath and, for the first time in what felt like forever, laughed.

"Finally!" he mused, a grin tugging at his lips. "And all it took was becoming the Oracle..."

EDICTS OF THE WISE

The Trusted Advisor: A Leader's Best Asset

A trusted advisor is more than an expert. They are the person leaders turn to when things go wrong. When standard strategies fail. When pressure is high. When decisions are unclear. They don't just give answers—they ask the right questions. The ones that cut through noise and reveal the real issue.

Unlike consultants or specialists, trusted advisors work on a different level. They don't just fix problems. They change how people see the problem. They challenge assumptions. They guide leaders to focus on what truly matters.

This isn't about being the smartest person in the room. It's about being the one who can handle uncertainty. A trusted advisor doesn't rush to solutions. They help others see clearly, so they can choose the right path themselves.

They don't need attention. Their power is in influence and understanding the way the dots join together. Their greatest strength? Seeing beyond the obvious. Recognising the real pain behind the symptoms.

Looking Past the Surface: Understanding the Real Problem

Most people mistake symptoms for problems. They focus on the obvious—bad processes, missed targets, poor performance. But these are just effects. The real cause is deeper.

A failing process may actually be a leadership issue.

A struggling team may have trust problems, not skill gaps.

A lack of results may come from unclear priorities.

Most people can't see the real issue. That's where a trusted advisor comes in. They listen. They observe. They uncover what's really happening.

Pain often hides in what's not being said. It's in the hesitation, the tension, the repeated problems. Great advisors don't rush to fix things. They take time to understand before they act.

The Right Questions Change Everything

A trusted advisor doesn't ask, "What's wrong?" That only gets surface-level answers. Instead, they ask:

"What happens if nothing changes?" (Forces leaders to face the cost of inaction.)

"What do you wish were true, but don't believe can happen?" (Reveals limiting beliefs.)

"Where do you feel resistance?" (Uncovers hidden fears.)

"If this problem disappeared, what would still be difficult?" (Prevents short-term fixes.)

"What conversation are you avoiding?" (Points to the real issue.)

The magic isn't just in the question. It's in how people struggle to answer. A trusted advisor watches for hesitation, body language, tone. Often, leaders already know the truth—they just haven't faced it yet.

Becoming a Trusted Advisor

You don't call yourself a trusted advisor. You earn it. Over time. Through action.

Listen deeply. Don't just hear words—read between the lines.

Build trust in small moments. Trust isn't built in one conversation. It grows through consistency.

Stay humble. It's not about being right. It's about being useful.

Push people beyond their comfort zone. Leaders don't need yes-men. They need people who challenge them with respect.

Be okay with uncertainty. Not every problem has a quick fix. Great advisors help others sit with complexity instead of rushing to easy answers.

The Guide, Not the Hero

A trusted advisor isn't the main character. They are the guide.

They don't seek credit.

They don't chase attention.

They measure success by how much they help others rise.

They influence without control. They lead without demanding followers. They ask the questions that shift thinking, change perspectives, and shape decisions.

That's why trusted advisors are the leaders of leaders. Not because they do the work—but because they help others think, see, and lead better.

True Influence Comes From Generosity

Influence doesn't come from authority. It comes from generosity. The best advisors don't hoard knowledge—they share freely.

They understand: the more you give, the more trust you earn.

They don't impose wisdom. They create space for others to discover their own insights.

They don't push their ideas. They ask questions that help others connect the dots.

They don't try to "win" conversations. They build understanding.

When people believe they came to an idea themselves, they commit to it fully. That's real influence. That's why great leaders don't give directives—they ask the right questions.

Mentorship as a Force Multiplier

Great leadership isn't about personal success. It's about making others better.

A trusted advisor doesn't just solve problems. They mentor. They empower. They build capability in others.

They don't keep people dependent. They teach them to think for themselves.

They don't just pass down knowledge. They sharpen other people's ability to navigate complexity.

They don't compete for influence. They create more leaders.

If your leadership doesn't outlive you, it was never real influence.

Generosity is a Strategy

Giving without expecting anything in return isn't just a virtue—it's a leadership strategy.

People trust those who give without an agenda.

The more you share, the more people value your input.

Leaders who give freely create networks of trust, respect, and loyalty.

Influence that relies on power fades. Influence that comes from trust and generosity grows.

Long-Term Influence, Not Short-Term Wins

Short-term wins are easy. Sustainable influence requires long-term thinking.

Don't chase quick fixes. Build frameworks that solve problems before they start.

Don't push people into compliance. Help them take ownership of ideas.

Don't just solve today's issues. Shape strategies and legacies that last.

Every conversation is part of a bigger picture. People will remember how you made them think, not just what you said.

Challenge the Thinking, Not the Person

People defend their ideas because those ideas feel personal. If you challenge the person, they get defensive. If you challenge the thinking, they stay engaged. A trusted advisor doesn't say, "You're wrong." They ask, "What if we looked at this differently?" The best influence doesn't come from confrontation—it comes from guiding others to see new perspectives without feeling attacked. Make it about the idea, not the ego.

Master the Pause—Sometimes Silence is the Best Question

Great advisors know when to speak—but more importantly, they know when to stop. Silence is uncomfortable, which is exactly why it works. When you ask a tough question, resist the urge to fill the space. Let the pause do its work. People rush to fill silence, and in doing so, they often reveal their real thoughts. The real insights don't come from rapid answers—they come from the moments people sit with discomfort and think deeply. If you want the truth, leave room for it to emerge.

Trusted Advisors Think in Systems, Not Just Situations

Most leaders focus on solving the problem in front of them. A trusted advisor looks at the pattern behind it. Is this a one-off issue, or is it part of a deeper system problem? Does this challenge keep repeating across different teams? Great advisors don't just fix problems—they uncover the hidden structures that cause them. Solving one issue is useful. Changing the system so it never happens again? That's leadership.

The Trusted Advisor's Path

True influence isn't about control. It's about trust.

The most effective advisors:

- » Ask better questions, not give more answers.
- » Help others think, not just tell them what to do.
- » Give generously, without keeping score.
- » Think beyond immediate results.

Trusted advisors don't seek power. They build capability in others. And in doing so, they create lasting impact.

They don't just lead people. They help others lead themselves

building a legacy of leadership, not just a following. This is the pinnacle—not just holding authority but creating leaders who can think, decide, and grow independently. The best leaders make themselves almost unnecessary because they've built something stronger than themselves—a culture where leadership keeps evolving.

Side Quest
Lessons Beneath the Stones

Arcanus had travelled far enough for the day, reaching the distance he'd set out to cover, when he spotted a group of explorers stranded near an outcrop of ruins. Curious and always willing to lend a hand, he steered his sand rider toward them. As he approached, he noticed a rope tied to their vehicle, hanging down into a deep hole—someone had either ventured inside or was about to.

A spectacled woman with a bushy mane of hair and an easy smile waved at him.

"Greetings, traveller!" she called.

Arcanus inclined his head with a warm smile. "Greetings. How may I assist you?"

"I'm Nessa, a scholar searching for lost historical artifacts. That's Bram—he's the one with the massive, curved sword—and over there is Eilo, our newly-graduated but untested mage."

Eilo blushed, mumbling into his beard. He was not much bigger than a child, but his impressive beard and weathered old-man face gave him a timeless appearance. A dwarf, Arcanus noted with interest. He'd known of them, but he'd never met one in person.

Bram, clearly growing impatient with the lack of action, shifted in place. Arcanus observed as the warrior spotted a small spider inching toward the rope, and with surprising precision, lobbed a wad of spit near it, startling the poor creature away. For all its crudeness, his aim was impressive.

"Pleased to meet everyone," Arcanus greeted, nodding to the trio.

After a brief round of introductions, Nessa explained their predicament: they had encountered an ancient doorway covered in glowing runes, and despite Eilo's magical knowledge, the meaning of the symbols remained beyond his expertise.

Arcanus, a little parched from the desert air, waved his hand, conjuring an ever-easy refreshment spell. A pot of steaming tea and a platter of pastries materialised, much to the delight of the group. As they sat together, sipping tea, Nessa enthusiastically dove into her passions, recounting tales of ancient civilisations, Bram's overprotective tendencies as her brother, and how they had saved Eilo, who now felt indebted to them and had joined their cause.

As the conversation settled, Arcanus rose, teacup in hand, and made his way over to the hole.

Within the Ruins

The ancient chamber was cool and dim, the air thick with dust. Before them stood an enormous stone door, glowing runes pulsing softly along its surface. Arcanus perched on a broken pillar, tea still in hand, observing the trio as they studied the inscriptions.

"What do you see?" he asked, gesturing to the runes with his teacup.

Bram grunted, arms crossed. "It's a warning. Maybe a curse."

"No," Nessa countered, tracing a faint pattern in the air. "They're instructions. Something about balance?"

Eilo, stroking his beard, nodded slowly. "A puzzle about harmony."

Arcanus smiled. "Exactly. Well done! Now, how will you solve it?"

Piece by piece, they debated, each contributing an insight. They experimented with different patterns, occasionally stepping back to reassess. Arcanus watched silently, sipping his tea, resisting the urge to step in.

Finally, after much discussion and a few accidental magical mishaps, the trio aligned the glowing runes correctly. The massive stone door groaned open, revealing a chamber filled with treasures—ancient scrolls, intricately crafted weapons, and golden trinkets untouched by time.

Nessa turned to Arcanus, her eyes alight with curiosity. "You knew the answer, didn't you? Why didn't you just tell us?"

Arcanus grinned, pulling out a tattered notebook titled: The Hitchhiker's Guide to the Unknown Realms.

"Because lessons learned last longer than instructions given," he replied, tapping the cover. "Always carry a good guide. And maybe a towel."

As they divided their spoils, Arcanus reminded them, "Treasure is not just wealth. Be generous and think long-term. A single coin, shared wisely, can multiply a hundredfold."

Later that night, under a sky strewn with stars, the adventurers sat by the fire, reflecting. They realised that what they had gained was not just gold, but the wisdom of collaboration and patience.

They left the ruins not only richer but wiser, their minds brimming with knowledge they would carry forward—and more importantly, share.

Side Quest
Reflections by Firelight

The travellers emerged from the darkness, drawn by the glow of Arcanus's campfire.

"Good travels, sir!" chirped a feminine voice. The speaker, a young woman, was hopping on one foot, grimacing in discomfort.

Arcanus inclined his head. "Hello, and good travels to you."

"May we share your camp? My feet are torn up," she continued, gesturing toward her boots, which had clearly seen better days.

"Of course. I may have something to ease the discomfort," Arcanus replied, reaching into his satchel. With a quiet whisper, he produced a "Pain No More" potion, palming it as if it had been sitting atop his supplies all along. He handed it to her discreetly—no need to startle them with conjuration.

The large man accompanying her—clearly a warrior—busied himself starting a fire without asking. Arcanus observed him for a moment but decided against making an issue of it. Instead, he offered a slow nod of approval, setting the group at ease.

They shared their rations, simple but filling, and for a time, the camp was silent except for the crackling of flames and the occasional sigh of exhaustion. The desert night stretched over them, vast and still.

A Fireside Reckoning

Tinker, the rogue, sat cross-legged, carefully rubbing the Pain No More potion onto her blistered feet. Arcanus saw the exact moment the potion took effect—the relief in her expression was unmistakable.

Nearby, Gareth the warrior ran a whetstone over his sword with slow, deliberate strokes. Arcanus watched him idly, reminded of Berik, and felt a pang of longing for his old companions.

Boggle the bard, meanwhile, hummed a familiar tune that sounded suspiciously like a nursery rhyme. Arcanus was about to retire for the night when he heard muttering—soft at first, then growing into grumbles. He let it continue, waiting for them to air their grievances.

When they fell silent, Arcanus leaned forward, resting his arms on his knees.

"You've all had your chance to grumble," he said, his tone dry as the desert dunes. "Now, tell me—what happened? How did this start, and what went wrong?"

The trio exchanged glances before Tinker sighed and relayed their misfortune:

A group of bandits, the Sand Sharks, had ambushed them and stolen their sand rider. Without it, they were stranded—trekking across the desert on foot was not only difficult but nearly impossible.

Arcanus stroked his chin thoughtfully. "Alright," he said, "what did we learn from this fiasco with the Sand Sharks?"

Tinker spoke up first. "The Sand Sharks are horrible, and we should avoid them at all costs?"

Arcanus raised an eyebrow.

She winced. "Alright, fine. I didn't scout far enough ahead

because I was trying to save time. I underestimated how much the terrain matters out here."

Gareth grunted in agreement. "And I assumed my strength alone would keep us safe. But brute force doesn't work when the ground is shifting beneath your feet." He tapped his sword against a rock. "Next time, I'll plan better for the environment."

Arcanus turned his gaze to Boggle, who was absentmindedly plucking at his lute.

"And you?"

Boggle cleared his throat. "I, uh, might've distracted us all with that improvised ballad about dune dancing..." he admitted, his face reddening. "Lesson learned: there's a time for art and a time to focus."

Arcanus nodded slowly, his expression unreadable. Then, he leaned forward and traced a pattern in the sand with his finger.

"What matters isn't the mistakes but the lessons you take from them, and how you use those lessons to grow." His tone softened, but the weight of his words settled over them. "Reflection leads to ownership. Ownership leads to improvement. And improvement leads to survival." His lips quirked into a faint smile. "Much like a certain wandering doctor once said: 'It's not the mistakes that matter, it's what you do next.' So... what will you do next?"

The group sat in quiet contemplation before murmuring their resolves—Tinker would scout farther ahead, Gareth would think smarter and plan for the environment, and Boggle would learn to balance focus with flair.

One by one, they settled into their bedrolls, the fire reduced to glowing embers.

Arcanus watched them drift into slumber, satisfied.

He exhaled, murmuring to himself, "Good. Another victory."

Then, with a small flourish, he pulled a peculiar, spinning contraption from his satchel. It emitted a soft, familiar hum as he whispered,

"Now, where did I put that sonic spanner?"

He chuckled to himself before vanishing into the shadows.

MASTERS OF THE MULTIVERSE:
Leaders from the Legends You Love

Indiana Jones (Indiana Jones) – The Reluctant Trusted Advisor

"It's not the years, honey, it's the mileage." – Indiana Jones doesn't just collect artifacts; he uncovers truths, deciphers hidden meanings, and challenges assumptions. He doesn't hand people answers—he forces them to think, to connect the dots, and to see beyond the surface.

Like a true trusted advisor, Indy thrives in uncertainty, navigating complexity without needing a perfect plan. He blends deep expertise with real-world adaptability, proving that knowledge alone isn't enough—what matters is how you apply it. He guides through discovery, not instruction, leading others to uncover the truth rather than dictating it.

A mentor in action, not in title, Indy teaches by doing, by questioning, by exposing risks others overlook. He empowers others to step up when it matters, not by controlling outcomes, but by creating the conditions where they can lead themselves.

Yoda (Star Wars) – The Trusted Advisor

"Do or do not, there is no try." – Yoda doesn't give answers; he challenges. He leads with wisdom, asks the right questions, and forces self-discovery. A true mentor on steroids, he guides Jedi to unlock their own potential rather than handing them solutions.

Gandalf (The Lord of the Rings) – The Guide, Not the Hero

"A wizard is never late, nor is he early. He arrives precisely when he means to." – Gandalf embodies the idea of influence without control. He doesn't force the Fellowship; he empowers them. His real power isn't in magic—it's in his ability to inspire and guide without dictating.

The Architect (The Matrix) – Understanding Systems, Not Just Problems

The Architect doesn't just look at symptoms—he sees the entire system at play. While cold and mechanical, he represents the need to think at meta-levels—beyond individual issues, into systemic causes and consequences. The trusted advisor operates similarly, helping others see the hidden structure behind problems.

The Doctor (Doctor Who) – Mentorship and Expanding Perspective

The Doctor never gives straight answers but asks the right questions to make people see beyond their immediate view. Time Lords don't just *know* things—they force others to expand their thinking. This is mentorship at its best—not dictating, but shaping perspective.

Data (Star Trek: TNG) – The Power of Continuous Learning

Data constantly seeks to improve—not just his knowledge, but his understanding of people. He embodies the culture of learning, ownership, and curiosity that great leaders and advisors instil. He doesn't just process information—he *reflects* on it, seeking wisdom beyond raw data.

Sherlock Holmes – The Master of Inquiry and Reflection

Holmes doesn't solve problems by *answering questions*—he solves them by asking better ones. He sees patterns, not just symptoms. This is the hallmark of a trusted advisor: seeing beyond the obvious and using inquiry to reveal deeper truths.

Spock (Star Trek) – Intellectual Humility and Logic with Empathy

Spock is the master of rational thinking, but his growth as a character shows the importance of balancing logic with emotional intelligence. A trusted advisor isn't just about being right—they're about being effective. Spock's best moments come when he blends wisdom with emotional awareness—the exact balance required for true influence.

THE UNWRITTEN RULES

Influence Comes More from How You Make People Feel Than What You Know

In technical fields, it's easy to assume that knowledge, logic, and expertise drive influence. But in reality, emotional connection and trust often matter more than the quality of your ideas.

Timing Matters as Much as the Message Itself

It's easy to assume that once you have a great idea or insight, you should share it immediately. However, in professional settings, when and how you present your thoughts can determine whether they are heard or ignored.

People Communicate in Layers—What They Say Isn't Always What They Mean

Literal interpretation can cause confusion. Many social interactions involve hints, emotions, or indirect meaning rather than direct words.

In mentorship and influence, understanding the emotion behind words can prevent miscommunication and deepen relationships

People Remember How You Show Up in Their Toughest Moments

Relationships aren't just built in fun times—they are often defined by how you show up when things are difficult.

When someone is going through stress, disappointment, or uncertainty, even a small gesture of presence, listening, or support can leave a lasting impact.

Many people assume that when others are struggling, they should give space—which is sometimes true. But just as often, people need to know that someone is there, even if they don't ask for it.

THE MIRROR OF MASTERY

» How comfortable am I with guiding people through questions rather than providing direct answers?

» Am I willing to focus on relationships and emotional intelligence, not just expertise and logic?

» Can I step back from being the expert and instead focus on long-term influence?

CHAPTER 9

We're All Weird

Main Quest

The Odyssey of Purposeful Leadership

Three months later

The grand hall of the Arcane Academy shimmered with an ethereal glow, the magyck-infused copper and glass reflecting the soft luminescence of suspended orbs above. The cathedral-like structure, adorned with intricate carvings of past wizards and shimmering semi-precious stones, stood as a monument to the finest minds in magyck. Tonight, however, the gathered assembly was abuzz with an air of unusual curiosity.

For tonight's honoree was not present—at least, not in the way they had all expected.

The recipient of the Academy's highest honour was none other than Arcanus Mylar, a wizard from humble beginnings, a name now whispered with reverence, confusion, and—among some—disbelief.

The Ceremony Begins

The hall's glow deepened as the final guests took their seats, robes of deep blue, silver, and gold rustling softly. The assembled wizards—young apprentices, seasoned scholars, and the Academy's elite—watched as the High Elder rose to his feet and took centre stage.

His presence was commanding, though his robe, heavy with the embroidered sigils of the greatest wizards in history, swayed lightly with each step. A monocle, ever his signature, hung from a fine chain over his heart. With a quiet breath, he placed it over his eye, a gesture that carried weight and seriousness.

Then, he spoke.

"Everyone, please take your seats—the ceremony will now begin."

A hush settled over the crowd as the rustling of robes and last murmurs of anticipation faded.

"Distinguished colleagues and guests, we gather tonight not only to honour a wizard but to reflect on a life that has redefined what it means to serve.

Many of you know his name. Some of you knew him personally. But tonight, we acknowledge what he has become.

Arcanus Mylar came to us from a minor noble family—a lineage that, in generations past, would have excluded him from even entering these halls. Many of you," his eyes swept over the assembly, "once scoffed at such origins, believing the wizarding arts should remain within the domain of wealth and prestige."

A pause.

A measured look.

"It is an ancient tradition I have fought against for years. A tradition that Arcanus himself shattered."

The murmurs that followed were not protests, but reflections—whispered acknowledgments of how the Academy had changed. How one wizard had changed it.

The High Elder continued.

A Life of Purpose

"Arcanus did not work hard because he had to. He was naturally gifted, with a rare intuition for magyck that rivalled even the most seasoned scholars. But he persevered—not for himself, but to show others that skill, dedication, and wisdom can come from anywhere.

He inspired, rather than demanded. Led, rather than commanded."

A thoughtful silence fell.

Then, the High Elder's voice deepened with gravity.

"Eighteen months ago, to this very day, I sent Arcanus on a mission—one that none of you knew of, for it required the utmost secrecy.

There were stronger wizards, yes. Master wizards with centuries of experience. And yet, I chose him.

Why? Because skill alone does not make a great wizard. It is the integrity of one's soul."

The weight of those words pressed into the hall.

"Arcanus did not merely succeed in his mission—he did something far greater.

He healed what was broken."

The crowd gasped, soft murmurs rippling through the assembly like a wave.

The High Elder raised a hand, and silence resumed.

The Redemption of Rafe Velisthane

"You have all heard the name Rafe Velisthane," the High Elder continued. "The fallen wizard. The terror of Darsura. The lost brother of the Arcane Order.

Arcanus did not see him as an enemy to be vanquished, but as a soul who had fallen—one that could yet be saved.

And so, he gave Rafe something many of us would not.

A second chance."

The murmurs resumed, this time in awe.

"It was through Arcanus's mercy, his wisdom, and his belief in redemption that Master Wizard Velisthane stands with us again today.

And Rafe—" the High Elder turned his head slightly, his eyes fixing on a hooded figure at the edge of the hall "—has kept his word. He has spent these past months not only undoing the destruction he wrought but aiding the High Council in ways only he could.

In time, he will take a seat among us once more."

The hooded figure of Rafe Velisthane slowly lowered his hood, revealing a man who had once been a shadow of himself—now whole again.

Some in the crowd looked away. Some nodded solemnly. But none dared to protest.

Because the proof of his redemption was standing before them.

The Final Gift of Arcanus Mylar

The High Elder took a deep breath.

"Arcanus returned the Oracle to its rightful home. He restored peace to Darsura. He walked the length of Raghan's unforgiving deserts and survived challenges that none of us could have foreseen.

And in the end, he did something… that none of us could have predicted."

He looked around the grand hall, his silver eyes glinting.

"He became something more."

Silence. Absolute silence.

A whisper of magyck curled through the hall, and the air shifted—hummed.

And then—

A blinding white light appeared.

It hovered just above the floor, pulsing with the brilliance of a thousand stars, shifting and forming into something almost human—but not quite.

The air itself seemed to bow in reverence.
And the gathered wizards gasped in understanding.
The High Elder smiled.

"I knew, even then, that he had been training for something far greater than any of us realised."

He turned to the glowing figure, and bowed.

"Welcome home, Oracle."

> "The future belongs to those who can see that the mass market is fading, and that weirdness is taking its place."
>
> "The world has been pushing us to fit in, but the new world demands that we stand out."
>
> "We are no longer constrained by geography, tradition, or the limits of mass production. We are free to be who we are."
>
> "The industrial revolution made 'normal' desirable because it was efficient. But efficiency isn't what moves us forward anymore—uniqueness is."
>
> — Seth Godin, We Are ALL Weird

> "The greatest risk is not uncertainty— it is the illusion of certainty."
>
> "The biggest mistake leaders make is assuming they have more control than they actually do."
>
> "The world is not a machine to be predicted, but a story to be interpreted."
>
> — John Kay, Mervyn King, Radical Uncertainty

The hall trembled with anticipation as the whispers of wizards, scholars, and dignitaries swirled like an unseen tempest. The sheer weight of the revelation—that the Oracle lived once more, and that Arcanus Mylar had become its vessel—was almost too much for the assembled crowd to absorb.

For centuries, the Oracle had been little more than a legend, a lost relic of wisdom and power. And now, through Arcanus, it had returned.

The High Elder, standing at the grand podium beneath the luminous crystal chandeliers, raised his palm for silence. It took several attempts before the murmurs and exclamations finally subsided.

Then, in a voice filled with reverence, he continued.

A Sacrifice Beyond Measure

"Yes," he confirmed, "Arcanus Mylar was tasked with returning the Oracle stone to its rightful place. And once there, he was given a choice. A choice that few, if any, would have been able to make."

The High Elder's gaze swept over the crowd, his silver eyes glinting in the candlelight.

"To become one with the Oracle is not merely an honour. It is not merely a title.

It is a sacrifice beyond measure."

A hushed silence gripped the room.

Every wizard knew what it meant to accept the mantle of the Oracle.

A wizard could become a master of elements, a keeper of runes, even a High Elder—but all of these still allowed a wizard to live a life. To love. To grow old.

But to become the Oracle?

To bind oneself to knowledge eternal?

That was to surrender oneself to duty for all of time.

It was a path of enlightenment—but also one of isolation.

A burden shouldered alone.
And Arcanus Mylar had accepted it willingly.

A Wizard Who Became Legend

The High Elder took a steadying breath, his expression shifting from solemn to proud.

"Arcanus Mylar has always given himself in service to others—not for reward, nor recognition, nor power, but because he believed in the work of making the world better.

And when the time came for the greatest decision of all, he proved, once again, that his commitment to his people, his City, and his Kingdom knew no bounds."

His voice, deep and steady, echoed through the hall.

"He stepped forward, as he always has.

He chose to bear the weight of history, so that we might continue to learn from it.

And tonight, we honour him—not just as the Oracle, but as the friend, the leader, and the soul who has changed our world forever."

A long, heavy pause.

Then— a toast.

"TO ARCANUS MYLAR!"

With a flourish, the High Elder lifted his goblet, his expression a mixture of pride and sorrow, his heart swelling for the friend he had known and the legend that had now transcended them all.

The Hall of Wizards Erupts in Tribute

As if the entire Academy had been holding its breath, the moment the High Elder's words ended, the hall erupted into a resounding chorus of cheers.

Glasses clinked. Robes rustled. Apprentices and masters alike rose to their feet, heads bowed in respect.

From the highest balconies to the most esteemed guests, every wizard in attendance raised their glass in salute.

They knew.

This was the last time Arcanus Mylar would ever be spoken of as "one of them."

Because tonight, he became something more.

A guardian of wisdom.

A keeper of histories.

An eternal guide.

A being whose name would be whispered for generations not as a wizard, but as the Oracle itself.

And somewhere, beyond the veil of time, where mortal eyes could no longer see, Arcanus watched.

He saw the friends he had left behind.

He saw the High Elder smiling with bittersweet pride.

He saw Berik, raising a tankard with a knowing smirk, as if to say, 'You really had to go and one-up us all, huh?'

He saw Sorche and Isla, clutching hands and whispering, their bond strengthened by all they had overcome.

He saw Juju, tears sparkling in his elven eyes, as he plucked out the first few notes of a ballad that would one day be sung across the world—the Ballad of the Oracle.

And as the celebration rang through the halls of the Arcane Academy, Arcanus Mylar—the wizard who had become legend—smiled.

Somewhere, deep in the cosmos, a star pulsed in quiet tribute.

Three months after the Award ceremony we catch up with Berik, Sorche and Juju.

The afternoon sun cast a warm glow over the training yard as Berik and his adopted son, Arry, clashed their wooden swords with playful energy. The rhythmic clack-clack of their blades echoed across the courtyard, mingling with the boy's excited laughter.

Berik, ever the warrior, observed the lad closely, pride swelling in his chest. Arry was quick. He was learning to read his opponent, his young feet moving in careful circles, seeking an opening. The boy had the makings of a fine fighter, and more than that—he had the spirit of one.

Berik had never imagined himself as a father. The life of a warrior was one of battle and bloodshed, not gentle teachings. And yet, fate had given him a second chance. A family. A purpose beyond the battlefield.

All thanks to Arcanus.

At the thought of his friend, his smile faltered.

It had been months—too many months—since he had last seen the wizard. His letters, once returned with replies full of wit and wisdom, had gone unanswered. There was no word, no trace of Arcanus anywhere. It was as if he had simply... vanished from the world.

Berik exhaled heavily, placing a scarred, calloused hand over his heart. He did not pray often, but in this moment, he closed his eyes and whispered:

"Be well, my friend, and enjoy your new life. All is as it should be."

And then—a whisper on the wind.

"All is as it should be."

Berik's eyes snapped open. His breath hitched.

That voice.

Arcanus.

He spun around, scanning the yard, his warrior's instincts on high alert. But there was nothing—no one. Just the rustling of leaves in the cool breeze.

Had he imagined it?

Was it just the wind?

Before he could dwell on it further, a sharp pain shot up his shin.

WHACK!

Berik let out a strangled grunt, staggering back as Arry's wooden sword landed a perfect strike against his leg.

The boy beamed with triumph, his arms raised high. "Got you good, didn't I, Da?"

Berik blinked down at his son, still half-lost in thought. But as he looked at Arry's proud, beaming face, the weight on his chest lifted. A deep, belly-shaking laugh rumbled through him, even as he clutched his throbbing shin.

He nodded miserably, hopping on one leg. "Aye, lad. You got me good."

Arry giggled in delight, already lunging in for another playful strike.

Berik raised his sword just in time, shaking his head with a grin.

Perhaps Arcanus was gone from this world.

Perhaps he was somewhere beyond Berik's reach now.

But wherever he was, Berik felt it in his bones:

His friend was at peace.

And for now—that was enough.

Several thousand miles away

Sorche sat at her desk, meticulously organising Juju's upcoming performances, grouping them efficiently to minimise travel time and maximise earnings. The bard was in high demand, and though he thrived in chaos, Sorche preferred order and structure. Her careful scheduling ensured that Juju's whirlwind lifestyle didn't spiral into complete anarchy—or at least, not more than usual.

She smiled as she overheard the familiar sound of Isla's voice, animatedly chatting with Juju about his latest performance costume. Isla, a talented seamstress, had a natural eye for design, and Juju relished her expertise.

"This one," Isla was saying, holding up a deep emerald doublet adorned with intricate gold stitching, "will make you shine under stage lights."

Juju twirled dramatically. "Darling, I always shine. But I do approve of a little extra help."

Sorche shook her head in amusement, grateful for this life they had built. Thanks to Arcanus, she and Isla had not just survived—but thrived. They had work they loved, a place they called home, and friends who felt like family.

Before she could get too sentimental, Juju bounced into her view, his usual mischievous grin firmly in place.

"Sorche, dearest, put down your dreaded planner for a moment and join us at the pub. I need my handler to witness my brilliance off the stage as well." He waggled his eyebrows. "I may even compose a ballad in your honour."

Sorche hummed and hawed, pretending to deliberate. She had been working all day, and truth be told, an evening out did sound tempting.

Juju pouted dramatically. "Sorcheee, live a little."

Finally, she sighed, rolling her eyes. "Fine. One drink."

Juju cheered triumphantly just as a familiar voice echoed through the room.

"One must lead a balanced life, Sorche. You have earned this, so enjoy it!"

Sorche froze. Her breath caught in her throat.

She whipped around—"Arcanus?!"—but saw nothing.

Only the soft rustling of papers on her desk.

Her heart pounded as she scanned the room, but there was no one there.

Just the faintest whisper of warmth lingering in the air.

"Sorche, you coming?" Isla popped her head into the office, oblivious to her sister's sudden stillness.

Sorche took a steadying breath before flashing a grin, shaking off the strange moment. "Aye, I have to see after you troublemakers."

She playfully tugged Isla's braid, earning a laugh from her sister.

"Come on! I hear there's a brand-spanking-new ale for us to try!" Juju whooped, grabbing both their hands and dragging them along toward the pub.

Sorche allowed herself to be pulled into the night, the laughter, the warmth of good company.

And as they walked beneath the glow of the lanterns, she swore she felt Arcanus's presence just beyond the veil of the ordinary—watching, smiling, and ever the wise friend.

> *"The people who thrive are not those who avoid uncertainty, but those who develop the ability to navigate it."*
>
> *"Successful people aren't the ones who chase every trend, but those who double down on what makes them unique."*
>
> *"In an unpredictable world, adaptability is the real superpower."*
>
> — Morgan Housel, Same as Ever

"The future will reward clarity but punish certainty."

"Success in leadership is not about having all the answers but about asking the right questions."

"Resilient leaders will embrace change as a continuous journey, not a single moment of adaptation."

— Bob Johansen, The New Leadership Literacies

1 year after the Recognition Ceremony

My dearest friends

I have 'looked' in on you, and I'm so pleased at seeing you well and happy, walking your path and relishing every moment. I am so proud of each, and every accomplishment you have achieved since our parting. You have turned your sorrows and tragedies into strengths and made them work for you, and that has made you resilient in a way that cannot be taught.

Each of you are unique souls: insightful, compassionate, humorous and with a wonderful outlook on life, souls that don't fit the norm — and have often struggled here and there trying to conform. You have grown, matured in that you no longer see the need to 'fit' in— by acknowledging who you are and what you want, you have broken free of the constraints that keep so many of us chained to the ordinary and the average, and that is something to celebrate.

I've always thought that seeing the world differently was a gift; most people don't see it as such, but I'm happy that you, my friends, finally do.

Stepping up to take control might not be something you've thought of. Perhaps you've faced situations where you were thrust into a position of leadership and wondered how to do this. Remember, each of us has a leader within, and someday we may all have to play this part in one form or another. Whether you're ready to accept that role remains to be seen, just know that it is within you to succeed in any position – all you need do is set your mind to it.

I've learned so much, and I wish you could view this world through my eyes, and see all the wonderfully weird, colourful folks like you who make up the fabric of the world. I wish you could see all the world and understand that you are not alone and have more allies out there than one can imagine. You, my friends, must find your tribe, yes, find your people, connect and create your own opportunities. Celebrate being different, celebrate being unique and live life to the fullest! Each and every one of you is special in your own way – never forget that!

Remember me, as I remember you.
Your loving friend once and always,

Arcanus

P.S. Come and visit at your soonest. Sorche and Juju, I know you will appreciate the wonderful oasis and all it offers. Berik, I think the monks here will give you a run for your money. They are insanely talented warriors and look forward to challenging the best warrior I know!

EDICTS OF THE WISE

This is Where It All Comes Together

This isn't a neat conclusion. It's a challenge.

This book was never about following a template for leadership. It's about recognising that real leadership comes from stepping into who you are. It's about using your strengths. It's about moving forward, even when the way isn't clear.

The world doesn't need more cookie-cutter leaders. It needs people who see what others miss. People who can handle uncertainty and still find clarity. That's the power of thinking differently. That's the power of being you.

Leadership isn't just for those at the top. It's for the team member who keeps everything running. It's for the manager juggling priorities. It's for the specialist who masters their craft. It's for anyone who steps up to make a difference, in whatever way they can.

Leadership is an Action, Not an Identity

Leadership isn't something you are—it's something you do. It's not about titles, confidence, or charisma. It's about actions, choices, and impact. Some of the best leaders never call themselves one. They just show up, take responsibility, and make things better. If you're waiting to feel like a leader before you act, you're thinking about it backward. Leadership isn't about a specific personality or skill set—it's about stepping in when something needs to be done.

The Leaders We Need, See the World Differently

The leaders of the future won't be the ones who fit the mould. They'll be the ones who break it. The ones who see patterns where others see chaos. The system thinkers, the deep technical minds, the logical problem-solvers, the ones who understand complexity instead of running from it. Leadership isn't just about standing in front of people and inspiring them with words—it's about understanding how the pieces fit together and making the right moves before anyone else sees them coming. If you think differently, that's not a weakness. That's exactly what makes you the leader we need next.

Leadership Isn't About Being Ready— It's About Showing Up Anyway

No one wakes up one day and just 'feels' ready to lead. That's a myth. If you're waiting for confidence before you step up, you'll be waiting forever. Leadership isn't about certainty—it's about making decisions in uncertainty. It's about stepping into the unknown, making the best call you can, and figuring it out as you go. The people who make a difference aren't the ones who waited until they were fully prepared—they're the ones who acted, learned, adapted, and kept moving. You don't need to be 'ready.' You just need to start.

You Don't Need to Change Who You Are

One of the biggest mistakes people make? Thinking they have to change to lead.

They believe leadership is about playing a role. About acting a certain way to fit some outdated image of authority.

But that's not leadership.

Leadership is about knowing yourself. It's about leaning into your strengths, recognising your weaknesses, and finding ways to work with both. It's about building self-awareness, trusting your instincts, and understanding that you don't need all the answers—you just need to be willing to figure them out.

Leadership Is About Taking Responsibility

Over my career, in my life, in service and volunteering, one truth stands out.

Leadership isn't about a title. It's about stepping up. It's about taking responsibility. It's about making things happen.

It's standing in the gap when no one else will.

The world changes because of people who refuse to wait. People who see a need and take action. Not because they have authority. But because they care.

Live Fully. Step In. Step Up.

I don't believe we are meant to sit back and wait. I believe we are called to live fully.

That means stepping into who you are right now. It means taking action, making decisions, and responding to the world as the person you are today.

It's not about waiting for permission. It's about realising you already have everything you need to start.

It Won't Be Easy. But It Will Be Worth It.

I won't pretend this road is easy. It's full of uncertainty. You will face challenges. You will fail. You will question yourself. You will reset.

And then? You will keep going.

Because leadership isn't about never falling. It's about learning. Not just learning skills. Learning who you are. Learning how you work best. Learning how to navigate a world that doesn't always make sense.

<u>Some of us don't fit into society's expectations. That's not a flaw. That's an advantage.</u>

The world is shifting. Old rules are breaking down. Success isn't about following a rigid path anymore. It's about adaptability, insight, and being bold enough to lead your own way.

You Don't Need Permission to Lead

If you take one thing from this book, let it be this.

You don't need to wait for a promotion. You don't need someone to tell you it's your time. You don't need to change who you are.

Leadership isn't about rank. It's about influence. It's about making things better. It's about stepping up when something needs to be done.

Forge Your Own Path

Life—and leadership—is not about finding the easiest road.

It's about creating your own.

It's about understanding that failure is part of the process, but resilience is a choice.

It's about surrounding yourself with people who challenge and support you. It's about building trust, credibility, and relationships so that people follow—not because they have to, but because they believe in what you're doing.

The Future Belongs to Those Who Step Up

The future belongs to those who refuse to be boxed in.

It belongs to those who know that leadership isn't about being the loudest. It's about being the clearest.

It's about knowing when to push and when to hold steady.

Final Questions

Will you lead?

Not the way the world expects. But in the way that is true to you.

Will you lean into your strengths? Will you own your quirks?

Will you use them to create something that matters?

Because the world doesn't just need more leaders.

It needs you. Fully. Unapologetically. You.

> "I am a leaf on the wind. Watch how I soar."
> — Hoban Washburne, Firefly

THE UNWRITTEN RULES

How People Hear You Matters More Than What You Meant

What you say and what people hear aren't always the same thing. You may intend to be efficient, honest, or precise, but others might interpret it as blunt, dismissive, overly critical, or rude. If your focus is on details, others may assume you're ignoring the bigger picture. Social cues aren't always obvious but recognising how people react can help you adjust how you communicate—without changing who you are.

Relationships Open More Doors Than Talent Alone

Being highly skilled is valuable, but opportunities often come from the connections you build—not just your expertise. Promotions, trust, and leadership roles don't always go to the most capable person; they often go to the person others feel confident working with. It's not about playing office politics—it's about creating strong, reliable working relationships.

Even if networking feels unnatural, small efforts to connect with people can have a big impact on future opportunities. But let's not be delusional—sometimes, politics will decide who moves up. When that happens, stand firm in your integrity, focus on your impact, and be the leader others respect. The best leaders don't always get the first promotion—but they're the ones people remember when things fall apart.

Your Work Only Counts If People See It

Hard work doesn't always speak for itself. Leaders and decision-makers don't have time to notice every detail of what you do. That doesn't mean self-promotion—it means making sure the right people see the impact you're having. If you're leading, solving problems, or driving results, make it easy for others to recognise. Share updates, connect your work to the bigger picture, and don't let your contributions get buried in the noise.

And real leadership isn't just making your own work visible—it's noticing the work of others. Call it out. Recognise contributions. Give credit where it's due. The best leaders don't just get seen—they make sure their team gets seen too.

People Won't Always Say What They Think— Watch for Unspoken Signals

Honest Feedback Isn't Always Direct, just because no one is giving you feedback doesn't mean they don't have thoughts. Some people avoid conflict, hesitate to give criticism, or hold back their real opinions—especially in group settings. Pay attention to tone, hesitation, or changes in behaviour. If people suddenly stop asking for your input or seem hesitant in conversations, something might be off. The best leaders don't just listen to words—they notice what isn't being said and create space for honest conversations.

THE MIRROR OF MASTERY

» How does my unique way of thinking give me an advantage in situations where others struggle?

» What is one part of myself that I have been hesitant to fully express, and what would change if I embraced it completely?

» How can I build a life where my uniqueness isn't just accepted, but truly valued?

When This Book Isn't for You

Not everyone will connect with this book. And that's okay. Maybe you read through it and found it unsettling. Maybe the way it moves, the way it frames leadership or the way it challenges traditional thinking doesn't sit right with you. That's completely fine. Not every perspective is for everyone.

But before you set it down, I want to leave you with two thoughts.

First—The World Has Told You Who to Be. Have You Ever Questioned It?

Many of us spend our lives shaped by expectations—by family, by workplaces, by society. We're given a "normal" version to follow, a mould we're supposed to fit into. And for some, that works. But what if it doesn't?

What if the way you think, the way you process, the way you lead doesn't match the blueprint you were given? What if your strengths don't fit into the categories others expect? What if the things that make you different aren't flaws but the very things that set you apart?

Whether you approach the world through faith, logic, science, or intuition, there comes a point where you may ask yourself: Are you being true to yourself? Have you really taken the time to understand how you think, how you grow, and what your place in the world truly is?

Because leadership isn't just about climbing a ladder—it's about stepping into who you are.

Second—Maybe This Book Feels Different. That's By Design.

For some, this book will resonate deeply. For others, it won't. And that's the point.

The old models of leadership—the rigid structures, the predictable paths, the industrial-era thinking—are breaking down. The world is changing fast, and leadership needs to evolve with it. The leaders who will shape the future aren't the ones who follow a set formula. They are the ones who see patterns others miss, who think deeply before they act, who know how to navigate complexity rather than just control it.

This book isn't about giving you a perfect roadmap to leadership. It's about starting the adventure. It's about giving people—especially those who think differently—a way to step forward and lead without having to fit into an outdated mould.

If That's Not You, Then What's Your Role?

Maybe you don't see the world this way. Maybe you don't feel like leadership has to change. Perhaps you prefer things structured, defined, and clear-cut. That's okay—not everyone is wired to lead in this way.

But here's the thing: these leaders already exist. They are in your teams, in your networks, in your communities. And too often, they go unnoticed. They don't seek the spotlight. They don't follow the traditional paths. But they are the ones who will shape the future.

So, I'll leave you with one last question:

Are you paying attention to them?

What are you doing to recognise, support, and empower the people who don't fit the old mould but are already shaping something new?

Because leadership isn't just about where you're going.

It's about who you're bringing with you.

CHAPTER X

Waystones of Thought in the Librarians Hoard

No great idea stands alone, like a lone traveller in the wilds. Ideas are forged in the heat of experience, tempered by the challenge of the journey, and woven together into something truly extraordinary.

Here lies a treasured collection of tomes and scrolls—wisdom from those who have ventured before, shaping this adventure in ways both visible and unseen. You may find them just as valuable on your adventure.

Of course, this is but a fraction of the vast library of knowledge, battle-tested theories, and fireside tales that have influenced this work. The full map includes countless unsung guides—mentors, conversations, research papers, and unexpected moments of insight. But for those seeking waystones of wisdom, this list is a worthy place to begin.

Adams, S. (1996) *The Dilbert Principle: A Cubicle's-Eye View of Bosses, Meetings, Management Fads & Other Workplace Afflictions.* New York: Harper Business.

Arbinger Institute. (2000) *Leadership and Self-Deception: Getting Out of the Box.* San Francisco: Berrett-Koehler Publishers.

Brown, B. (2018) *Dare to Lead: Brave Work. Tough Conversations. Whole Hearts.* New York: Random House.

Carnegie, D. (2011) *How to Win Friends and Influence People in the Digital Age.* New York: Simon & Schuster.

Collins, J. (2001) *Good to Great: Why Some Companies Make the Leap... and Others Don't.* New York: HarperCollins.

Covey, S. R. (1989) *The 7 Habits of Highly Effective People: Powerful Lessons in Personal Change.* New York: Free Press.

Cunningham, K. J. (2017) *The Road Less Stupid: Advice from the Chairman of the Board.* Austin: Lioncrest Publishing.

Duke, A. (2018) *Thinking in Bets: Making Smarter Decisions When You Don't Have All the Facts.* New York: Portfolio.

Duckworth, A. (2016) *Grit: The Power of Passion and Perseverance.* New York: Scribner.

Fowler, J. W. (1981) *Stages of Faith: The Psychology of Human Development and the Quest for Meaning.* New York: HarperOne.

Fowler, S. (2014) *Why Motivating People Doesn't Work... and What Does: The New Science of Leading, Energizing, and Engaging.* Oakland: Berrett-Koehler Publishers.

Frankl, V. E. (1946) *Man's Search for Meaning.* Boston: Beacon Press.

Ford, I. (2010) *A Field Guide to Earthlings: An Autistic/Asperger View of Neurotypical Behaviour.* Independently published.

Gates, B. (1995) *The Road Ahead.* New York: Viking.

Godin, S. (2007) *The Dip: A Little Book That Teaches You When to Quit (and When to Stick).* New York: Portfolio.

Godin, S. (2011) *We Are All Weird: The Myth of Mass and the End of Compliance.* New York: The Domino Project.

Godin, S. (2008) *Tribes: We Need You to Lead Us.* New York: Portfolio.

Goleman, D. (1995) *Emotional Intelligence: Why It Can Matter More Than IQ.* New York: Bantam Books.

Haddon, M. (2003) *The Curious Incident of the Dog in the Night-Time.* London: Jonathan Cape.

Harford, T. (2016) *Messy: How to Be Creative and Resilient in a Tidy-Minded World.* New York: Riverhead Books.

Harper, I. (2011) *Economics for Life: An Economist Reflects on the Meaning of Life, Money, and What Really Matters.* Melbourne: Acorn Press.

Heller, M. (2012) *The CIO Paradox: Battling the Contradictions of IT Leadership.* Boston: Harvard Business Review Press.

Hogarth, R. (2019) *Becoming King of the Nerds: A Guide to Leadership for the Intellectually Inclined.* Independently published.

Housel, M. (2023) *Same as Ever: A Guide to What Never Changes.* Harriman House.

Johansen, B. (2017) *The New Leadership Literacies: Thriving in a Future of Extreme Disruption and Distributed Everything.* Oakland: Berrett-Koehler Publishers.

Jones, D. M. (2020) *Autism for Adults: 50 Things You Need to Know.* Jessica Kingsley Publishers.

Kay, J. & King, M. (2020) *Radical Uncertainty: Decision-Making Beyond the Numbers.* New York: W.W. Norton & Company.

Kaufman, J. (2010) *The Personal MBA: Master the Art of Business.* New York: Portfolio.

Kotter, J. P. (2021) *Change: How Organizations Achieve Hard-to-Imagine Results in Uncertain and Volatile Times.* New York: Hachette.

Laraway, R. (2022) *When They Win, You Win: Being a Great Manager Is Simpler Than You Think.* New York: St. Martin's Press.

Lowndes, L. (2003) *How to Talk to Anyone: 92 Little Tricks for Big Success in Relationships.* New York: McGraw-Hill.

Macdermid, K. (2019) *Human-Centred Design for IT Service Management.* Independently published.

Martell, D. (2023) *Buy Back Your Time: Get Unstuck, Reclaim Your Freedom, and Build Your Empire.* New York: Portfolio.

Maister, D. H., Galford, R. & Green, C. (2001) *The Trusted Advisor.* New York: Free Press.

Meadows, M. (2017) *Grit: How to Keep Going When You Want to Give Up.* Independently published.

Newport, C. (2016) *Deep Work: Rules for Focused Success in a Distracted World.* New York: Grand Central Publishing.

Moore, M. G. (2019) *No Bullsh!t Leadership: Why the World Needs More Everyday Leaders and Why That Leader Is You.* Brisbane: James Kerr Publishing.

Priestley, D. (2010) *Key Person of Influence: The Five-Step Method to Become One of the Most Highly Valued and Highly Paid People in Your Industry.* London: Rethink Press.

Ross, J. W., Sebastian, I. M., Beath, C. M. & Mocker, M. (2019) *Designed for Digital: How to Architect Your Business for Sustained Success*. Cambridge: MIT Press.

Sinek, S. (2014) *Leaders Eat Last: Why Some Teams Pull Together and Others Don't*. New York: Portfolio.

Sinek, S., Mead, P. & Meyer, D. (2017) *Find Your Why: A Practical Guide for Discovering Purpose for You and Your Team*. New York: Portfolio.

Smith, M. J. (1975) *When I Say No, I Feel Guilty*. New York: Bantam Books.

Strom, M. (2014) *Lead with Wisdom: How Wisdom Transforms Good Leaders into Great Leaders*. Brisbane: Wiley.

Warren, R. (2002) *The Purpose Driven Life: What on Earth Am I Here For?* Grand Rapids: Zondervan.

Watkins, M. D. (2013) *The First 90 Days: Proven Strategies for Getting Up to Speed Faster and Smarter*. Boston: Harvard Business Review Press.

White, K. (2018) *The Shift: How Seeing People as People Changes Everything*. San Francisco: Berrett-Koehler Publishers.

The Holy Bible: English Standard Version. (2001) Crossway Bibles.

CHAPTER XX

The Real Arcanus

This book is the start of an interesting journey, one where you will not only learn more about yourself (the good, the bad and the oh-so interesting), but you will find out how to develop your assets, contain your liabilities, and become a more holistic version of yourself – where it counts.

At its core, this book is an adventure where you will demonstrate grit, perseverance, focus and more, and at the end, you will be the best version of you to date.

Why this book?

I discovered the term "neurodivergent" probably about eight years ago, and back then, it wasn't the buzzword it's become today. Discovering new perspectives about myself made a lot of sense because I was one of those people who really struggled in life. I was a very quiet person, loved keeping to my own devices and was, technically what you would call a "doer." I had my fingers in many pies, and unfortunately, that also meant I had to mingle with other people. Now, you might not understand what social savviness has to do with someone not running for office, but trust me – it does!

I'd look at social situations and puzzle, "What the hell is going on?" or I'd wonder, "Why can't we just get on with ____?" I didn't understand why one had to navigate the social scene instead of being direct and candid. Of course, what I didn't know back then was that *networking* plays no small part in deciphering the political and social animal that is part and parcel of our world.

I remember being a child who was vastly intrigued by the world of computers. Back in the day, we played around with all kinds of computers and gadgets – I was the kid working out how MS-DOS works, playing old-skool games and trying to take over the world, one keyboard stroke at a time. It was a delightful way of seeing something not only come to life, but also understanding what made it tick from the ground up. I was the type of individual who *learnt best by doing*, and it's something that has worked for me most of the time. On my leadership journey, I've needed to see what's going on and test it for myself, and I've done a lot of that since, I've never been a shoo-in for mentoring. No one ever volunteered to mentor me! I had to do a hell of a lot of observing - from the outside. It took a while to realise that people like myself needed to ask. I've been the outlier or oddball my entire life. At the same time, I was the person who observed everything, and that gave me great skill of insight that others failed to see and needed to know.

I must have been about eight, and visiting my aunt. I drew a wonderfully complex drawing of a machine that was across the road at the park. That machine basically pruned trees where the operator would take those trimmings, shred it and put it into the truck. The truck would then take it all the way to the depot. I just sat and watched the machine, noticing the fine details all the way down to the barricades, the warning, the flashing lights, the trees in the background and the workers. I noticed everything! No detail was too small or unimportant for my young eyes. My nan (grandmother) noticed and commented on my powers of observation. Fast forward decades later, and my analytical skill is something I pride myself on, a superpower that few have. Of course, like Superman has his Kryptonite, so do I.

What I *didn't* see or struggled to make out was the social inference (amongst many others) – if something's implied or inferred, it skips right over my head. Ever felt like you missed the first half of the movie? That was me... The relationships

I missed out on with kids my age was due to my inability to read the room – I struggled to fit in and was bullied constantly. I thought, "Hmm, perhaps I should copy the popular kids and do what they do," except it never really worked out, and I got into a ton of trouble…

I was often hit, pushed, and belittled. I tried to pretend like it didn't hurt my feelings, that I was invincible, but of course, being human meant that I felt everything (and deeply too). That didn't stop me from enjoying myself in my own way, but I knew that I couldn't play *their* game.

My mother had an *epiphany* and realised I was different after I finished high school, flopped on the couch and exhaled a long, grateful sigh, "Thank God that's over!!" She realised that while I was a bright kid, I didn't absorb knowledge in the same way as other kids. Being the remarkable woman she is, she was determined to find a way to help educate me in a way that stuck *and* encouraged me in discovering my unique path. I appreciated her efforts, especially as it made me realise, I was not alone. There were other kids just like me!

I moved on to tech college, and it was here that *I finally felt like I belonged*. I got to do things I really enjoyed around people who enjoyed it too, and that was equally important because I felt like I had found my people – people in the tech industry. For the first time in my life, I scored amazing grades. I understood what I was doing, and more than that, I enjoyed learning. I felt like this was the path I was meant to be on, an inspiring career I could look forward to.

Rather than a downhill ride, life has been a journey full of twists and turn. I have had and continue to have my share of challenges. There was the sexual abuse I endured as a kid, and while my memory of it is non-existent, there is no doubt that this affected me in some vital way. My family have been an amazing support system, rooted in faith and Jesus Christ. It meant that I understood hardships were meant to be shared so you could help others overcome their obstacles, inspire them to reach out and become mentors for others who needed you.

I have always been delighted to help people with computer-related issues, so my career was picked out for me in a way. I realised that the willingness and desire to help people was my main goal and tech was the tool I could wield to do so. In many ways, that's part of my book's motivation – sharing ideas and motivations through these different lenses for people that may be a bit like me!

Open to my career now. I've become and been a Head of IT and a Chief Technology Officer. I have had the amazing ability to work with such a tremendous number of diverse, interesting businesses and organisations throughout my entire career, and it has been a joy to see so many ideas come to life, and to witness the transformation of businesses and individuals in this digital era. I understand now that what started as a fascination with computers has become a tremendous opportunity. Now, I get to run my own business. It's not much, but it's something. I get to share the wisdom I've learned over the years with people, partnering with them to take advantage of and create the leverage they need to make better businesses and organisations in the digital era. But beyond that, ensuring we do not neglect or diminish what it is to be human. We must learn from the mistakes of the past, using these tools and instruments in wholesome, strong, and productive ways.

For people like us, we love our stories. I'm a big fan of Indiana Jones, The Lord of the Rings, Dilbert, Harry Potter, and The Big Bang Theory, to name a few. The whole idea of storytelling appealed to me when I decided to write this book.

I wanted an interesting way of helping others unlock their potential and I wanted to incorporate many of my favourites (and hopefully yours too). How many have you spotted?

My passion revolved around merging the technical aspect with a desire to help others, but how can *you* achieve this when the world plays by a different set of rules? So, that's what this book is: an adventure where you will demonstrate grit, perseverance, focus and more, and at the end, you will be the best version of you to date! You will be able to see the opportunity, and you will understand more of what that means as the journey unfolds.

I also needed to ensure we had fun with the story, while remaining serious about the overall goal: self-development in the emergent digital era.

Your questions and more are answered in the book as you engage in our quests (Yes! We have those) and read some fantastic quotes that give you food for thought. You will identify parts of your personality in our characters and discover what it takes to step up and take lead, venture into new lanes, and lead with influence – to be someone others look up to. This book is dedicated to the misfits, the oddballs, and the outsiders - the ones who are quietly brilliant in their own way and perhaps seek a *different* way to shine.

Let's go on that journey of self-discovery. You won't regret it – I promise!

www.ingramcontent.com/pod-product-compliance
Lightning Source LLC
Chambersburg PA
CBHW020356080526
44584CB00014B/1038